Later Modern Irish History: Topic 5

Case Studies: Politics and Society In Northern Ireland, 1949–1993

Anne-Marie Ryan

The Educational Company of Ireland

First published 2020
The Educational Company of Ireland
Ballymount Road
Walkinstown
Dublin 12
www.edco.ie

A member of the Smurfit Kappa Group plc

ISBN 978-1-84536-927-9

The paper used in this book comes from Managed Forests in Northern Europe For every tree felled, at least one new tree is planted

Layout: Carole Lynch
Editor: Sally Vince
Indexer and proofreader: Geraldine Begley
Cover photography: Getty Images

Acknowledgement is made to the following for supplying photographs and for permission to reproduce copyright photographs:
Alamy pp1, 2, 4, 5, 6, 7, 8, 9, 15, 16, 18, 19, 21, 22, 23, 26,27, 28, 29, 31, 32, 35, 47, 48, 49, 50, 51, 52, 55, 57, 59, 61, 73, 74, 75, 77, 78, 81, 82, 83, 93, 95, 110, 112, 115, 119, 121, 123, 125; Ardfern p93; Derry Journal p34; Getty Images pp cover, 10, 16, 24, 36, 37, 58, 59, 60, 76, 77, 78, 83, 85, 86, 87, 92, 95, 96, 105, 127; HMSO p84; iStock p51; National Library of Ireland pp6, 8, 32; National Museum of Northern Ireland pp11, 15; nicivilrights.org p108; National Portrait Library p25; Public Records Office of Northern Ireland pp53, 75; RTÉ Stills Library pp13, 17, 18, 33, 57, 82; Topfoto pp3, 11, 14, 15, 59; Victor Patterson pp28, 60, 92, 94, 96, 97.

The publisher would like to thank the following for text material:
British Council Ireland: p40; The British National Archives: pp84, 102; M E Collins: pp135-37; The Deputy Keeper of the Records, Public Records Office of Northern Ireland: pp41, 42, 45, 98; The Derry Journal: pp39, 43, 44, 65; Four Courts Press: p45; Gill Books: pp30, 89; Victor Gollancz (publisher): p72; Haymarket Books: p64; The Irish Press: p69; The Irish Times: pp39, 63, 71, 80; Nina Kent: p99; Londonderry Sentinel: p54; Methuen Publishing: p103; National Archives of Ireland: p100; O'Brien Press: p100; Orion publishing: p103; Royal Irish Academy: p90; The Times: p70; Times Books: p101; Ulster Society Publications: p66.

Web references in this book are intended as a guide for teachers. At the time of going to press, all web addresses in this book were active and contained information relevant to the topics in this book. However, The Educational Company of Ireland and the author do not accept responsibility for the views or information contained on these websites. Content and addresses may change beyond our control and pupils should be supervised when investigating websites.

Contents

Foreword

This book is designed to prepare students for the compulsory topic in the Leaving Certificate exam: the documents-based question. The question requires students to have an in-depth knowledge of three case studies and their wider historical context.

For 2022 and 2023 the compulsory topic that pupils are required to study is *Later Modern Irish History: Topic 5 – Politics and Society in Northern Ireland, 1949–1993*. The three case studies for this topic are:

» The Sunningdale Agreement and the Power-sharing executive, 1973–1974
» The Coleraine University controversy
» The Apprentice Boys of Derry.

Each of these case studies is dealt with in a separate section of the book. Chapters break down each topic into the main areas of study. Photographs and other forms of artwork are used to help students develop their visual sense of the period. Key terms are explained, and review questions allow students to assess what they have learned.

Knowledge of the wider historical context for the topics covered in the case studies will increase students' understanding and better prepare them for possible exam questions. For this reason, some historical background information is provided in two introductory chapters.

An important aim of this book is to develop students' ability to tackle the documents-based question in the Leaving Certificate exam. Students need to be able to extract relevant information, compare how two sources deal with a topic, detect bias, recognise propaganda, assess reliability and put the case study in its historical context. With this in mind, there are a number of sources with questions throughout the chapters. Importantly, each case study has three Leaving Certificate-style documents-based questions to familiarise students with the different question types to expect in the exam.

To aid students in their study and to allow them to investigate the different topics in more detail, a reading list of relevant books and websites is included. There is also a section focusing on key personalities and a detailed glossary that will aid understanding of some of the main terms and concepts that are involved in the different topics.

As a further aid to teachers and students, a series of presentations on the case studies can be accessed at www.edco.ie/lchistory and www.edcolearning.ie.

1 The creation of Northern Ireland and the early years of the state, 1920–1945

Statue of Edward Carson at Stormont

This chapter looks at events leading to partition in Ireland in 1920, resulting in the six counties in the north of Ireland becoming Northern Ireland, governed by a parliament in Belfast. The political and economic differences between the north and south of Ireland became marked and long-lasting after the Second World War.

Useful terms

▸ **Dominion status** According to the Anglo-Irish Treaty (1921), the newly created Irish Free State would be self-governing but would remain part of the British Commonwealth (empire).

▸ **Guerrilla warfare** Fighting by a small independent group, often against regular soldiers.

▸ **Internment** Imprisonment without trial.

▸ **Plenipotentiary** A representative of a government given full power to act as they see fit on behalf of their government, often when in a foreign country.

▸ **Republic** A state in which power is held by the people through their elected representatives, and which has an elected president rather than a monarch.

The creation of Northern Ireland in 1921 was the result of decades of political conflict in Ireland over home rule. Unionists living in the north-east of Ireland were strongly opposed to a parliament for Ireland that would be based in Dublin. The strength of their opposition almost led to civil war, which was prevented only by the outbreak of the First World War in 1914.

The Government of Ireland Act 1920 brought about the partition of Ireland in 1921, with the six counties in the north of Ireland governed by

> **? KEY QUESTION**
> What events led to the creation of the Northern Ireland state in 1921?

a parliament in Belfast. The first 20 years of Northern Ireland were dominated by prime minister James Craig, who aimed to strengthen unionist control of the state.

The outbreak of the Second World War was to have a lasting impact on Northern Ireland, widening the gap both politically and economically between the north and south of Ireland.

What led to the creation of the Northern Ireland State (1886–1921)?

Home Rule, 1886 and 1893

The major political issue in Ireland in the late 19th and early 20th centuries was **home rule**. Since 1801, Ireland had been part of the **United Kingdom of Great Britain and Ireland** and was governed directly by the parliament at **Westminster**.

Home rule was the campaign for Ireland to have its own parliament that would pass laws relating to the affairs of Ireland. Control of external affairs, such as foreign policy and the army, would remain with Westminster.

Unionists:
▸▸ Opposed to home rule. They felt British and wanted to maintain the union between Great Britain and Ireland.

▸▸ The vast majority of unionists were **Protestants**.

▸▸ Most unionists lived in the north-east of Ireland.

Nationalists:
▸▸ Supported home rule. They felt Irish and wanted greater independence for Ireland.

▸▸ The vast majority of nationalists were **Catholics**.

▸▸ Nationalists made up the majority of the population in Ireland but were a minority of the population in the north-east of Ireland.

Home rule was strongly opposed by **unionists**. Unionists in Ulster were against home rule because:

▸▸ They believed it would threaten their prosperity, in particular the thriving shipbuilding and linen industries of Belfast

▸▸ They feared a Dublin parliament under Catholic control.

Opposition to home rule in the 19th century was organised by the **Orange Order**.

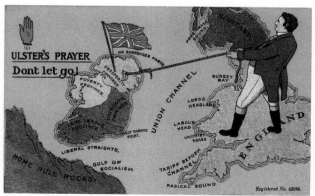

An anti-Home Rule Unionist Postcard: Ulster's Prayer – Don't Let Go! circa 1912

The **Orange Order** is a Protestant society. It was established in 1795. One of its main functions is to commemorate the victory of the Protestant king William of Orange over the Catholic king James II in the battle of the Boyne (1690). Parades are held annually on 12 July to commemorate this victory. The parades have frequently been associated with sectarian violence.

Home rule bills were introduced to the Westminster parliament in 1886 and 1893 but failed to become law. In 1893 the home rule bill was passed by the House of Commons but was **vetoed** (rejected) by the House of Lords.

Home rule crisis, 1912

Opposition to home rule in Ulster reached a high point in 1912. Following a general election, the **Liberal Party** under **Herbert Asquith** needed the support of the pro-home-rule **Irish Parliamentary Party** in order to form a government. In exchange for their support, Asquith agreed to introduce a third home rule bill to parliament.

Ulster Day, 28 September 1912

The House of Lords no longer had the power to veto a bill from the House of Commons and so the introduction of home rule to Ireland seemed likely. Opposition in Ulster was led by **Edward Carson**, the leader of the **Ulster Unionist Party** and **James Craig**. On **'Ulster Day'**, 28 September 1912, nearly half a million people signed the **Ulster Solemn League and Covenant**. They pledged that they would use 'all means which may be found necessary' to stop home rule.

Irish Volunteers

By 1914, Ireland seemed on the brink of civil war. The **Ulster Volunteer Force**, a volunteer army, was formed in January 1913. It obtained a significant number of weapons in April 1914, when guns were landed at Larne, Co. Antrim. In the south, the **Irish Volunteers** formed in November 1913 with the aim of defending the introduction of home rule to Ireland. The Irish Volunteers also acquired weapons when guns were landed at Howth in Dublin in July 1914.

The crisis was averted with the outbreak of the **First World War** in Europe in August 1914. Legislation for home rule was passed but it was not to be implemented until the end of the war.

First World War

Upon the outbreak of war, Carson ordered the Ulster Volunteers to enlist with the **British Army**. By the end of 1915 an estimated 28,000 Ulster Volunteers had signed up, forming the **36th (Ulster) Division** of the British Army. They participated in key battles, including the **battle of the Somme** in which 5,500 members of the division were killed or wounded in the first two days.

Edward Carson inspecting Ulster Volunteers

Easter Rising, 1916 and the rise of Sinn Féin

The events of the **Easter Rising** in 1916 were mostly confined to Dublin and did not have a direct impact on Ulster. However, the executions of the leaders of the rising and the **internment** of suspected rebels began to change public opinion in Ireland. Where previously nationalists had supported home rule, increasingly they supported an independent Irish republic.

Dublin Post Office shortly after Easter Rising, April 1916

Across Ireland there was a growth in support for **Sinn Féin**, which backed a policy of withdrawing Irish MPs from Westminster and setting up an independent national parliament in Dublin. In the general election of December 1918, Sinn Féin won 73 out of Ireland's 105 seats in the Westminster parliament. The Ulster Unionist Party won 23 seats in Ulster and were the largest party in that region of Ireland.

Government of Ireland Act, 1920

The landslide election victory of Sinn Féin and the outbreak of the War of Independence in 1919 meant that some form of self-government for Ireland was urgently needed to satisfy the demands of nationalists. It was evident, however, that unionists in Ulster would not tolerate being governed by an all-Ireland parliament based in Dublin.

The solution arrived at by the British government under prime minister **David Lloyd George** was the **Government of Ireland Act, 1920**, which created the **partition** of Ireland. According to the act:

» The six counties of **Antrim, Armagh, Down, Fermanagh, Derry** (then known as Londonderry) and **Tyrone** would be called Northern Ireland and be governed by a parliament based in Belfast.
» The Northern Ireland parliament could legislate on domestic issues such as education and agriculture but the Westminster parliament would still have control of taxation and foreign policy.
» According to **Section 75** of the Act, the Westminster parliament retained supreme (highest) authority over affairs relating to Northern Ireland.
» The remaining 26 counties of Ireland would be governed by a parliament based in Dublin.
» Twelve MPs would represent Northern Ireland in the Westminster parliament.

Map showing the partition of Ireland following the Government of Ireland Act, 1920

 KEY QUESTION
How did James Craig strengthen unionist control of Northern Ireland between 1921 and 1940?

Northern Ireland under James Craig, 1921–1940

Northern Ireland parliament

Elections to the new **Northern Ireland parliament** took place in April 1921 using a **proportional representation** system. The results were:

» Ulster Unionist Party – 40 seats
» Sinn Féin – 6 seats
» Nationalist Party – 6 seats

Unionist control of parliament continued for several decades.

James Craig

Proportional representation is an electoral system where voters can vote for their chosen candidates in order of their preference. A proportional representation system is considered fair, as parties win support in proportion to the number of votes cast for them by the electorate. It contrasts with the 'first past the post' system used in Westminster elections, where the candidate with the most votes in an election is automatically elected to parliament.

The parliament opened at Belfast City Hall on 22 June 1921. Only the Ulster Unionist Party representatives were present as the Sinn Féin and Nationalist Party representatives refused to take their seats in protest against partition. James Craig (Lord Craigavon) became the first prime minister of Northern Ireland.

James Craig opens the parliament

Anglo-Irish Agreement, 1921

The Government of Ireland Act was largely ignored in the south of Ireland. Sinn Féin had established an independent Irish parliament, **Dáil Éireann**, in 1919 and the **Irish Republican Army** (IRA) continued its campaign of **guerrilla warfare** throughout the early months of 1921.

In July 1921, a **truce** was agreed and from October to December of that year negotiations for a treaty settlement were held between **plenipotentiaries** sent by Dáil Éireann (led by Michael Collins) and the British government (led by Lloyd George).

A major sticking point in negotiations was the issue of partition. The division of Ireland was

The first Dáil Éireann, 1919

seen as unacceptable by Collins and his negotiators; however, the possibility of an all-Ireland parliament was outright rejected by Craig.

The **Anglo-Irish Treaty (1921)** created the **Irish Free State**: 26 counties in the south of Ireland that would have **dominion status**. As a compromise on the issue of partition, the treaty provided for the setting up of the **Boundary Commission** to decide on the Irish border. The Irish delegates were led to believe that areas of Northern Ireland with large Catholic populations would be transferred to the Irish Free State.

Michael Collins, centre, with the Treaty makers, 1921

Sectarian violence

There had been a growth in **sectarian** tensions since 1920, after rioting broke out in Belfast when Catholic workers were expelled from the shipyards. The activities of the IRA across Ireland and the changing political situation led to sectarian violence in 1921 and 1922. The violence took the form of house burnings, evictions, kidnappings, rioting, assassinations and bombings. The situation was particularly acute in Belfast and border areas. It reached crisis point in the first six months of 1922, when 171 Catholics and 93 Protestants were killed.

> **Sectarianism** The division between religious groups. It can take the form of prejudice, discrimination or hatred towards a particular religion. In Northern Ireland, sectarian divisions have occurred between the Protestant and Catholic communities.

The **Special Powers Act (1922)** was introduced in an effort to end the violence. The act contained some extreme measures, which included giving the newly established police force, the **Royal Ulster Constabulary**, the power to arrest and intern suspects without trial. Under the act, the **minister of home affairs** had the power to make organisations illegal and to ban parades. It was intended as temporary, emergency legislation but it was made permanent in 1933.

Members of the IRA, 1921

British troops in Ireland during the War of Independence, 1920

Boundary Commission, 1925

The setting up of the Boundary Commission in 1925 resulted in little change to the border. The six counties in the north-east of Ulster remained as Northern Ireland. This resulted in a population that was approximately two-thirds Protestant and one-third Catholic. Many of the policies pursued by the unionist governments in the following decades were aimed at strengthening unionist control of Northern Ireland.

Members of the Boundary Commission, 1925

Craig: 'A Protestant parliament and a Protestant state'

During a debate in the Northern Ireland parliament in 1934, Craig emphasised the Protestant character of Northern Ireland. He described himself as 'an Orangeman first and a politician and Member of this Parliament afterwards' and went on to declare that 'we are a Protestant Parliament and a Protestant State'.[1]

James Craig (standing centre, wearing a badge on his lapel) with members of the Ulster Unionist Party in 1912. Many of those pictured became ministers in James Craig's government

In the first decade of the existence of the Northern Ireland state there was evidence of a consolidation (strengthening) of unionist control in Northern Ireland. The Protestant population in Northern Ireland remained fearful of the Catholic minority in Northern Ireland and the majority Catholic population in the south of Ireland. The creation of a '**Protestant State**' was a form of defence against this perceived threat.

Orange Order parade, 1922

Control was strengthened in a number of areas, mainly:

» Political control
» Law and order
» Public service employment.

Political control

Local elections were held in Ireland in 1920. Following the introduction of partition, unionists were in control of two-thirds of councils in Northern Ireland and nationalists were in control of one-third. Although unionists held a majority of the councils, many of the councils under nationalist control refused to recognise partition or the Northern Ireland parliament. This was a matter of concern for the unionist government.

In 1922, proportional representation was abolished. This system of voting was considered to favour the Catholic minority. An **electoral commission** was set up to review local government boundaries. It received submissions only from unionist parties and as a result boundaries were redrawn in a manner that favoured unionist election candidates. In the local elections that followed, nationalists lost control of councils such as **Derry Corporation** and the county councils of Fermanagh and Tyrone. Nationalists accused the unionist government of **gerrymandering**.

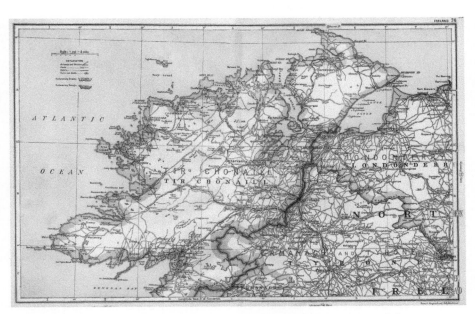

Map (1936) showing Co. Donegal (Tír Chonaill) in the Irish Free State and the bordering counties of Derry, Fermanagh and Tyrone in Northern Ireland

Gerrymandering is where the borders of electoral areas are redrawn in a way that suits the interests of a particular group. It is used to enable a smaller political group to obtain a victory over a larger political group. In Northern Ireland, gerrymandering was used in areas where there was a majority nationalist population. Electoral borders were manipulated in such a way that unionist candidates could win control of local councils and be elected to the Northern Ireland parliament.

The situation was particularly acute in the city of Derry. In 1936, there were further changes made to the boundaries of **electoral wards** in the city. As a result, in the local election that followed, 7,500 unionist voters elected 12 councillors to the city corporation and 10,000 nationalist voters elected 8 councillors. Therefore, control of the corporation was in unionist hands even though the city had a majority nationalist population.

In the late 1920s proportional representation was also abolished for elections to the Northern Ireland parliament. The result of the election to the Northern Ireland parliament in 1929 was that Craig's Ulster Unionist Party won 37 out of 52 seats. Nationalists held only 15 seats and formed such a small opposition that many nationalist politicians stopped attending debates in parliament. During elections, in constituencies where there was a clear unionist majority, nationalists did not put forward any candidates to contest the seat.

Law and order

In October 1920, the **Ulster Special Constabulary** (USC) was formed to counteract the activities of the IRA in the north. It included a reserve force commonly known as the **B-Specials Division**. This was an exclusively Protestant division and its first members were mostly former members of the Ulster Volunteer Force (UVF).

The **Royal Ulster Constabulary** (RUC) was established in April 1922 to replace the Royal Irish Constabulary (RIC) that had previously been responsible for policing in Ireland. Rank-and-file membership of the force was never less

RUC officers on patrol in Belfast in an armoured car, 1935

than 90 per cent Protestant. By the late 1920s, there were 3,000 RUC officers. It was supported by the reserve force of the B-Specials, which numbered 12,000.

Members of the judiciary were almost all Protestant and many judges were closely associated with the Ulster Unionist Party.

Public service employment

Another way in which unionist control in the governing of Northern Ireland was strengthened was through employment in the civil service. Civil servants working for the government of Northern Ireland after 1921 were mostly from the Protestant community. The minister of home affairs, **Dawson Bates,** held particularly sectarian views and refused to employ any Catholics in his ministerial office.

Economy

The economy of Ulster had thrived in the late 19th and early 20th centuries. This was largely due to the success of the shipbuilding and linen industries. The shipyard of **Harland and Wolff** was located in Belfast and in 1890 employed 10,000 men. The **York Street Flax Spinning and Weaving Company,** also in Belfast, was the largest factory of its kind in the world.

The shipbuilding and linen industries received a boost from an increase in demand for their products during the First World War. However, this demand collapsed once the war was over and Northern Ireland experienced an economic downturn in the 1920s. On average, the unemployment rate was 19% of the workforce between 1923 and 1930. The global economic recession prompted by the **Wall Street Crash** in 1929 led to severe unemployment rates in the 1930s. An average of 27% of the workforce was out of work between 1931 and 1939.

Harland and Wolff shipyard, Belfast

How was Northern Ireland affected during the Second World War?

The British prime minister **Neville Chamberlain** declared war on Germany on 3 September 1939. The following day, Craig declared in the Northern Ireland parliament (which had been located at **Stormont** since 1932) that 'the Ulster people' were 'prepared ... to face all the responsibilities' that being in a state of war entailed.

At first, the Second World War had a limited impact on Northern Ireland. In November 1940, having suffered ill health for some time, Craig died in office. He was succeeded as prime minister by **John Andrews**, who faced the greatest challenge of the war in April and May 1941. Two major air raids were carried out by the **Nazis** in Belfast, resulting in the deaths of 1,100 people and damaging 56,000 homes.

Andrews proved ill-equipped to handle the difficulties of wartime government and in 1943 he was replaced as prime minister by **Basil Brooke**.

Belfast air raid damage

Impact of the Second World War on Northern Ireland

During the Second World War, the relationship between Northern Ireland and Great Britain was strengthened as the strategic importance of Northern Ireland became clear. With its access to the Atlantic, Derry was used as the main port for fuelling the **destroyers** that protected convoys of ships travelling between America and Britain. As many as 300,000 **American soldiers** were stationed in bases in Northern Ireland during the war as they awaited transfer to the front lines.

The war helped to bring an end to the poor economy of the 1930s. The shipyards and aircraft industry experienced a boom period and there was a huge increase in tillage output.

The contribution of Northern Ireland to the war effort contrasted with the policy of **neutrality** in the south of Ireland. While the northern economy grew during this period, the economy of the south experienced a period of stagnation. Overall, a significant outcome of the Second World War was a widening of the gap – both politically and economically – between the north and south of Ireland.

REVIEW QUESTIONS

1	Why were unionists living in Ulster against home rule?
2	During the home rule crisis in 1912, what was 'Ulster Day'?
3	In 1914, why did it seem like Ireland was on the brink of civil war?
4	What event prevented the outbreak of civil war in Ireland in 1914?
5	How did the Easter Rising, 1916 change the attitudes of nationalists in Ireland?
6	Outline the key points of the Government of Ireland Act, 1920.
7	Why were only Ulster Unionist Party representatives present at the opening of the Northern Ireland parliament on 22 June 1921?
8	Who was the first prime minister of Northern Ireland?
9	Explain how a compromise was reached on the issue of partition during the negotiation of the Anglo-Irish Treaty, 1921.
10	Describe the increase in sectarian violence in Northern Ireland in 1921 and 1922.
11	What measures were included in the Special Powers Act, 1922?
12	What was the outcome of the Boundary Commission, 1925?
13	Explain the term gerrymandering as it applied to Northern Ireland in the 1920s and 1930s.
14	Explain how measures introduced in the area of law and order served to increase Protestant control of Northern Ireland.
15	Which industries were most successful in Ulster in the late 19th and early 20th centuries?
16	What was the average rate of unemployment in Northern Ireland between 1931 and 1939?
17	What happened in Belfast in April and May 1941?
18	Who replaced John Andrews as prime minister of Northern Ireland in 1943?
19	What was one of the main outcomes of the Second World War for North–South relations?

2 Northern Ireland: the origins of the Troubles, 1945–1969

CIVIL RIGHTS MARCH

Civil rights march in Newry, November 1969

This chapter shows how for a period after the Second World War there was peace in Northern Ireland. However, reforms introduced in Westminster gradually caused discontent in Northern Ireland, culminating in violence in the 1960s that signified the beginning of the Troubles, which continued for decades.

Useful terms

▸ **Franchise** The right to vote in an election.

▸ **Infrastructure** Facilities such as roads, airports and energy supplies that help businesses and factories to function.

▸ **Loyalist** A more extreme type of unionist. Loyalists strongly support the union between Great Britain and Northern Ireland and have a firm attachment to Protestant and British cultural heritage.

▸ **Republican** A more extreme type of nationalist. Republicans believed that the situation in Northern Ireland could be resolved only by the end of partition and the creation of a thirty-two county Irish republic. Many republicans were willing to use violence in order to achieve this.

The period between the end of the Second World War and the outbreak of the Troubles in the late 1960s was peaceful. Some of the reforms introduced by the postwar Labour government in Westminster and the Unionist government in Belfast in the 1940s and 1950s would sow the seeds of discontent that would emerge in the 1960s and tensions began to emerge between the Protestant and Catholic communities. A growing sense among the Catholic community that they were

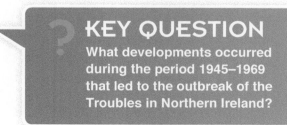

? KEY QUESTION
What developments occurred during the period 1945–1969 that led to the outbreak of the Troubles in Northern Ireland?

experiencing discrimination in areas such as housing and voting rights led to the formation of the civil rights movement in the late 1960s. The eruption of violence during civil rights protests marked the beginning of decades of violent conflict in Northern Ireland known as the Troubles.

What was Northern Ireland like under Basil Brooke, 1945–1963?

Basil Brooke became prime minister of Northern Ireland during the Second World War. Throughout his time in office he maintained unionist control of the Northern Ireland government.

The coming to power of a **Labour** government in Britain in 1945 posed difficulties for the Ulster Unionist Party, which did not traditionally support left-wing policies. However, they were reassured by a strengthening of the connection between Northern Ireland and the United Kingdom in 1949, when the Labour government passed the **Northern Ireland Act**. This stated that Northern Ireland could not leave the United Kingdom without the consent of the Northern Ireland parliament.

Basil Brooke (1888–1973), prime minister of Northern Ireland

The welfare state

Like the rest of the United Kingdom, Northern Ireland benefited from social reforms in the areas of welfare, healthcare and education that were introduced by the Labour prime minister **Clement Attlee** in the aftermath of the Second World War. Benefits such as **free healthcare** and **free second-level education** were extended to Northern Ireland in the late 1940s.

Of particular significance was the **Education Act**, introduced in 1947. This made free secondary school education available to all children over the age of 11 and grants were made available to those wishing to access higher education. Many individuals who would later play a key role in the civil rights movement (see p. 16), including **John Hume** (see chapter 4) and **Bernadette Devlin** (a civil rights leader and politician; see p. 110), benefited from the education they received as a result of the welfare state.

Housing

The **Northern Ireland Housing Trust** was set up in 1945 to provide public housing. By the early 1960s, 100,000 houses had been built by the trust. Most of these new houses were allocated to individuals and families by local authorities. This system led to accusations of discrimination in the late 1960s, when it was argued that local authorities tended to favour Protestants over Catholics in the distribution of housing.

Economy

The traditional industries of shipbuilding and linen went into sharp decline in the 1950s, due to a decrease in demand and competition from other countries. Unemployment rates in Northern Ireland were often double the UK average during this decade. The **Hall Report** (1962) recommended that the government should try to attract foreign investors to set up factories and businesses in Northern Ireland, instead of trying to develop existing industries.

In 1963, Basil Brooke (who was now Lord Brookeborough) was aged 74 and had been in office as prime minister for twenty years. He was considered incapable of introducing the modern economic policies needed to improve the standard of living for people in Northern Ireland. He was replaced as prime minister by **Terence O'Neill** in March 1963.

Weavers working in a linen factory in Northern Ireland in the 1950s. After the Second World War, the linen industry went into decline

What was Northern Ireland like under Terence O'Neill, 1963–1969?

On taking office as prime minister, O'Neill declared that the aim of his government would be to 'transform Ulster'. In O'Neill's view, the two key areas in need of reform were:

» The economy
» The relationship between the unionist and nationalist communities in Northern Ireland.

Terence O'Neill (1914–1990), prime minister of Northern Ireland

O'Neill aimed to modernise the Northern Ireland economy by improving **infrastructure** and by providing **financial incentives** that would attract foreign investors to establish businesses in Northern Ireland. To a large extent he was successful in these aims:

» New motorways were built
» Construction began on a new city (called **Craigavon** after James Craig) located south of Belfast
» Foreign companies, such as **Goodyear** and **Grundig**, set up operations in Northern Ireland.

The construction of motorways formed an important part of economic development in Northern Ireland. This is an aerial view of a section of the newly constructed M2 motorway, 1973

Another stated aim of O'Neill was 'to build bridges between the two traditions within our community'. During his years as prime minister, O'Neill made frequent visits to Catholic schools and hospitals. In January 1965, there was a significant improvement in **north–south relations** when the Taoiseach, **Seán Lemass**, met with O'Neill at Stormont. O'Neill made a return visit to Dublin the following month.

Terence and Katharine O'Neill with Kathleen and Seán Lemass on the occasion of O'Neill's visit to Dublin in 1965

O'Neill made significant progress in the areas of the economy and relations with the nationalist community. In spite of this, O'Neill's time in office coincided with a period of growing discontent, particularly among the nationalist community. Long-held grievances over **discrimination** against the Catholic community came to the fore in the late 1960s. This gave rise to the **civil rights movement**, a campaign for political and social reforms in Northern Ireland.

Origins of the civil rights movement

In the late 1960s, a large section of the nationalist community in Northern Ireland felt that they were being discriminated against in a number of key areas:

» Housing
» Gerrymandering
» 'East of the River Bann' policy
» Employment.

Housing

There was evidence of discrimination in the allocation of **local authority housing**. In Fermanagh, for example, approximately two-thirds of houses were allocated by the council to Protestants and one-third was allocated to Catholics, even though a majority of the population were Catholic.

The condition of some housing was poor, particularly in Derry, where there were problems with overcrowding and the condition of many houses was deemed unfit for human habitation.

View of the Bogside, Derry in 1960. Issues relating to the condition of housing, overcrowding and discrimination in the allocation of public housing caused controversy in the 1960s

Gerrymandering

The policy of gerrymandering (see p. 9) continued. Electoral boundaries were maintained in such a way that unionists won a majority of seats in elections, even in areas where there was a majority nationalist population.

In 1966, the nationalist population in Derry outnumbered the unionist population 2:1. In spite of this, local government elections that year resulted in 8 nationalist and 12 unionist councillors being elected. Gerrymandering was largely responsible for this, but it was also because **voter franchise** in local elections was limited to **householders who paid rates** (council tax). The restriction on voter franchise disproportionately affected nationalist voters who were less likely to be householders than unionist voters.

'East of the River Bann' policy

The nationalist community felt that the vast majority of economic investment in Northern Ireland was being directed to the eastern region of Northern Ireland. They believed that the western region, where there was a large Catholic population, was being neglected in favour of the mostly Protestant east. Approximately 70% of the new factories that set up in Northern Ireland during the O'Neill years were located **east of the River Bann**.

In 1965 the decision to locate a second university for Northern Ireland in **Coleraine** instead of Derry (see case study, chapters 3 and 4) was seen as further evidence of the neglect of the western region.

Employment

In the 1960s it was still the case that the vast majority of senior positions in the civil service were held by Protestants. In the private sector, Catholics 'were more likely to be found in industries with lower status and more unemployment, such as construction'.[1] Protestants dominated the more skilled industries, such as engineering and shipbuilding. It was also the case that Catholics were more likely to be unemployed than their Protestant counterparts.

The foundation of NICRA and the growth of the civil rights movement

The **Northern Ireland Civil Rights Association** (NICRA) formed in January 1967 with the aim of campaigning to end practices that discriminated against Catholics. One of their popular slogans was '**one man, one vote**' which highlighted the limited franchise in local elections.

The first civil rights march was held in August 1968, when 2,500 people marched from **Coalisland to Dungannon** to protest against discrimination in the allocation of housing in Co. Tyrone. The marchers were confronted by approximately 1,000 members of the **Ulster Protestant Volunteers**, who were supporters of the **loyalist** leader **Ian Paisley**.

Austin Currie organised the first civil rights march from Coalisland to Dungannon in 1968

Another march was organised for Derry on 5 October 1968 by the **Derry Housing Action Committee** and NICRA (see also case study chapter 6, The Apprentice Boys of Derry, 1949–1993). In spite of a ban on parades from the **minister of home affairs William Craig**, the civil rights protestors went ahead with their march. During the march they were confronted by police who used water cannon and batons to disperse the protestors. The events were captured by **RTÉ** cameraman **Gay O'Brien** and the footage of police officers mistreating the marchers was broadcast around the world.

RUC officers during the civil rights march in Derry, 5 October 1968

O'Neill's five-point programme

O'Neill came under growing pressure from the British government under Labour prime minister **Harold Wilson** to introduce reforms. Terence O'Neill announced a **five-point plan** to address the demands of the civil rights movement. This included replacing **Derry Corporation** with an independent commission to run the city and using a **points system** to allocate housing.

On 9 December 1968 O'Neill made a television address to the people of Northern Ireland. He declared that '**Ulster stands at the crossroads**' and called on the civil rights marchers to end their protests while reforms were being introduced. He also asked the loyalist opponents of the marchers to show restraint.

Burntollet Bridge, January 1969

Attack on Burntollet Bridge

Bernadette Devlin was one of the main organisers of the People's Democracy march that was attacked at Burntollet Bridge. She was elected MP to the Westminster parliament in April 1969

In response to O'Neill's plea, many within the civil rights movement stopped protesting to allow time for reforms to be introduced. However, a group called **People's Democracy** decided to hold a march from Belfast to Derry, starting on 1 January 1969. People's Democracy was made up of students, mostly from **Queen's University Belfast**; **Bernadette Devlin** was a prominent member.

On the fourth day of the march, at **Burntollet Bridge**, the marchers were ambushed by a group of loyalists who threw stones, glass bottles and iron bars at the protestors. Off-duty members of the **B-Specials** were among those who attacked the marchers. News of the treatment of the marchers at Burntollet Bridge led to rioting and demonstrations across Northern Ireland.

Resignation of O'Neill

The situation continued to deteriorate in the early months of 1969. Increasingly, civil rights demonstrations were controlled by more extreme **republicans** and became more violent.

In an **election to the Northern Ireland parliament** in March 1969, 27 out of the 39 unionist MPs elected were pro-O'Neill. After the election, however, O'Neill continued to lose support from within his own party. On 22 April, he agreed to introduce the reform of 'one man, one vote', allowing all citizens over 18 to vote in local elections. The following day his cousin and fellow Ulster Unionist Party MP **James Chichester-Clark** resigned in protest.

James Chichester-Clark

A series of bombing attacks were carried out on electricity power stations and water pipelines in late March and early April. These attacks were blamed on the IRA, although it was later uncovered that loyalist extremists were responsible. The attacks led some members of the Ulster Unionist Party to turn away from O'Neill. They believed the policy of introducing reforms was not bringing calm to the growing state of tension in Northern Ireland. With his supporters deserting him, O'Neill resigned as prime minister of Northern Ireland on 28 April.

The origins of the Troubles – conclusion

No one had predicted the violent eruption of conflict between Catholics and Protestants that occurred in Northern Ireland in 1968 and 1969. Nonetheless, tensions had existed for generations between the two communities and had been exacerbated by postwar developments in Northern Ireland, outlined in this chapter.

The case studies explored in the chapters that follow illustrate both the causes and the course of the period that became known as **the Troubles**:

» **Chapters 3 and 4: The Coleraine University controversy** explores how the controversial decision in 1965 to locate a second university for Northern Ireland in Coleraine contributed to the formation of the civil rights movement.

» **Chapters 5 and 6: The Apprentice Boys of Derry** explores how the activities of the Apprentice Boys of Derry provoked growing tensions between Protestant and Catholic communities in Derry and contributed to the beginning of the Troubles in August 1969.

» **Chapters 7–9: The Sunningdale Agreement** explores the attempt to find a political solution to the growing conflict in Northern Ireland in the years 1972–1974.

REVIEW QUESTIONS

1	Why were members of the Ulster Unionist Party concerned by the coming to power of a Labour government in Britain in 1945?
2	Explain how Northern Ireland benefited from the welfare state in the late 1940s.
3	What was the conclusion of the Hall Report (1962)?
4	Outline the successes of Terence O'Neill's economic policy.
5	How did O'Neill attempt to 'build bridges' with the nationalist community?
6	Give an example of discrimination in the area of housing in Northern Ireland in the 1960s.
7	Why was voter franchise in local elections seen as particularly unfair?
8	What was the 'East of the River Bann' policy?
9	What happened at the first civil rights march in 1968?
10	Why was the film footage of the October 1968 civil rights march so significant?
11	What were the main points of O'Neill's 'crossroads' speech in December 1968?
12	What happened at Burntollet Bridge in January 1969?
13	Why was Terence O'Neill forced to resign in April 1969?

CASE STUDY A:

The Coleraine University Controversy 1960–1965

3 The origins of the Coleraine University controversy, 1960–1965

Magee College, Derry

Free secondary education for children meant more students were going on to higher education. The Lockwood Committee was tasked with assessing post-secondary school needs, but went beyond their remit and recommended that a new university be built in Coleraine. However, this angered many people who believed that Derry was a better location.

Useful terms

» **Higher education** Education that takes place after secondary school at a university or college.

» **Cabinet** A group of senior government ministers and the prime minister who meet regularly to discuss government policy and make decisions.

A growing student population accessing university education was the main reason why a second university was needed for Northern Ireland by the 1960s. The Lockwood Committee was set up to investigate the higher education needs of Northern Ireland. Although the committee was not charged with choosing a location for a second university, it made the controversial recommendation that a new institution be established in Coleraine. This caused outrage in Derry, where local people believed their city was a more appropriate location for the university.

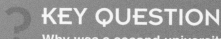
KEY QUESTION
Why was a second university needed for Northern Ireland and how was a location for that university decided upon?

Why was a second university needed?

By the 1960s it became clear that a second university was needed for Northern Ireland. There were two main reasons for this:

- A growing population was accessing third-level education
- The need to provide education in technological areas to create a skilled workforce that would attract investment to Northern Ireland.

The benefits of the welfare state

As with the rest of the United Kingdom, Northern Ireland benefited from the social reforms introduced by the **welfare state** after the Second World War (see also p. 14). The **Education Act (Northern Ireland) 1947** guaranteed free secondary school education for all children over the age of 11 and raised the school leaving age to 15. The act had a huge impact on the number of students participating in the education system: between 1947 and 1964 the total population of school-going children increased by 40%.

As a consequence of the growing numbers attending secondary school, more students were progressing to third level. This was made possible by grants for third-level education provided for under the Education Act.

The only university in Northern Ireland was **Queen's University Belfast**. Projections showed that numbers attending the university would double between 1960 and 1970. However, expansion of the university was limited by the city-centre location of Queen's as the surrounding lands were already built on or were too expensive to acquire.

Queen's University Belfast

Economic development and the Wilson Report

Another factor in establishing a second university was the need to equip young people with the technological skills that would attract foreign companies to locate in Northern Ireland. The **Wilson Report**, an ambitious plan for the development of Northern Ireland published in 1965, highlighted the need for a second university to facilitate economic growth.

Why did Derry want Northern Ireland's second university?

From the early 1960s, Derry was being put forward as a location for a second university in Northern Ireland. In March 1960, the Nationalist Party MP **Eddie McAteer** raised the matter with the then minister of finance **Terence O'Neill** in the Stormont parliament, asking him to consider the possibility of 'providing full facilities for university education in Londonderry city in view of the large and growing student-potential of the NorthWest'.[1]

Neglect of the north-west

In 1963, Derry Corporation published a submission making a case for a university to be located in their city. The corporation argued that locating a university in Derry 'would help to restore the equilibrium of Northern Ireland, educationally, economically and culturally'.[2]

At this point, many people in Derry – in particular the nationalist community – felt that the economic development of their city was being neglected. There were a number of reasons for this:

View of Derry, 1966

» The **Matthew Report** (1962) had recommended that a 'new city' be established in Northern Ireland. People in Derry were disappointed by plans to locate the city to the south-west of Belfast, as they felt the development of their city would be neglected as a result. The decision to call the 'new city' Craigavon, after the first unionist prime minister of Northern Ireland James Craig, was viewed as further evidence of Protestant bias in the economic policy.

» It was felt that economic investment in Northern Ireland was being concentrated in the eastern half of the province, where there was a majority Protestant population. This was borne out by the **Wilson Report** (1965) where it was mainly regions in the east that were identified as centres for economic development.

People in the north-west region felt increasingly isolated because of the closure of railway lines to Derry in the 1950s and 1960s. A final straw was the announcement of the closure of the Derry–Portadown line in 1965.

Magee College, Derry

Another factor considered to favour Derry as a location for a second university was that there was already a higher education institution, Magee University College, usually referred to as **Magee College** (founded in 1865 as Magee Presbyterian College), located in the city. It was thought that this college could be incorporated into a new university.

When it started, the main area of study at Magee was theology, but the college expanded over the years to provide a broader range of subjects. Magee could not award degrees but had an arrangement with Trinity College Dublin whereby students could complete their degrees at that university. The college remained small, however, and by the 1960s suffered from a lack of income, cramped conditions and declining student numbers.

Why was the Lockwood Committee set up?

The Stormont government set up a committee to investigate the future requirements for higher education in Northern Ireland. This was modelled on the **Robbins Committee**, a British government-appointed committee whose recommendations in 1963 led to a huge expansion of university education in Britain.

Formation of the Lockwood Committee

The **Lockwood Committee** was appointed in December 1963. It was chaired by **Sir John Lockwood** and consisted of seven men and one woman, four of whom were from England and four of whom were from Northern Ireland. There were no Catholic members on the committee.

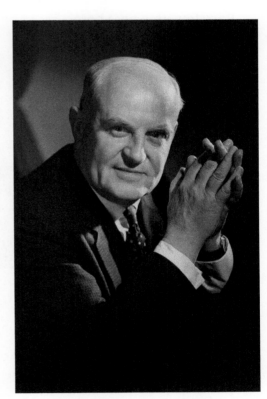

Lockwood was master of Birkbeck College, London and had experience in establishing universities in west Africa and Asia. The three other English appointees were academics from British universities. There were two representatives from industry in Northern Ireland: Brum Henderson, the managing director of **Ulster Television** and Denis Rebbeck, the managing director of **Harland and Wolff** shipbuilding company. The final two appointees were a grammar school headmaster, and a former civil servant of the Ministry for Education at Stormont.

Sir John Lockwood, master of Birkbeck College, who was appointed chair of a committee in 1963 to investigate higher education needs in Northern Ireland

Lockwood Committee: choosing a location for a second university

The main objective of the committee was to outline the broader higher education needs for Northern Ireland. Initially, it was not required to identify a location for a second university, but by the second meeting of the committee it became clear that Queen's could not expand any further. The need for a second university was now obvious and the focus of the committee shifted towards proposing a suitable location for this university.

Four possible locations for a second university in Northern Ireland emerged: **Derry**, **Coleraine**, **Armagh** and the proposed **'new city'**. Derry and Coleraine soon became the strongest contenders. The 'new city' was dismissed as a location, as building work had not yet started on the project and its planned location was considered too close to the existing university in Belfast. Armagh was also near Belfast and its population was considered too small to justify locating a university there.

Coleraine and Derry presented detailed proposals to the Lockwood Committee outlining the benefits of their town as the site of a new university.

The Coleraine proposal

Coleraine appealed to the Lockwood Committee for several reasons:

1 There were two potential sites for a university.
2 Extensive student accommodation was available in the nearby seaside towns of **Portrush** and **Portstewart**, where hotels could be used as student residences during the off-season. This would save money on building costs.

One reason why the Lockwood Committee favoured the Coleraine proposal was because of its proximity to the seaside towns of Portrush and Portstewart, which could provide student accommodation outside the tourist season

3 The town's location near the coast, the River Bann and Lough Neagh would benefit the establishment of a marine biology department, which was planned for the second university.

The River Bann at Coleraine

The Derry proposal

The Derry proposal emphasised the potential for Magee College to form the basis of a new university. In contrast to Coleraine, however, the Lockwood Committee found a number of disadvantages in the Derry proposal:

1 No site for the university was identified.
2 There was not enough detail provided on student residences and it seemed that students would mostly be accommodated in rented rooms in private houses.

As illustrated by this photograph of the Coyle family outside their home, the condition of housing in Derry was poor in the 1960s. Lack of suitable accommodation was one reason why the Lockwood Committee rejected Derry as a location for a new university

3 On visiting Magee College, the Lockwood Committee identified poor communications between the teaching staff and the governing body of the college.
4 Magee College had a **Presbyterian** ethos. The committee was concerned that this could cause difficulties if Magee was to become the second university, as students from all religious backgrounds would be attending.

Magee College

Based on points 3 and 4 above it was decided that Magee could not form part of the new university.

The city of Derry was still considered as a possible location; however, as the deliberations of the Lockwood Committee went on it became clear that the committee was leaning towards Coleraine. Problems with housing conditions in Derry were well known and expensive student accommodation would have to be built if the university was to locate in the city. At a meeting in May 1964 the committee heard that industrialists considered Derry to be too isolated a location to set up business; this was considered the final setback in the case for locating the second university there.

What were the recommendations of the Lockwood Report and the government's response?

Key recommendations of the Lockwood Report

On 16 December 1964, a memorandum was presented to cabinet by the minister of education, Herbert Kirk, which outlined the key recommendations of the Lockwood Report:

1 Higher education should be available to everyone in Northern Ireland, based on academic ability.
2 A second university was needed for Northern Ireland due to the increase in numbers accessing higher education and the inability of Queen's to expand any further.
3 The second university should be located in Coleraine.
4 Magee College should cease to exist as a university institution and no longer receive government funding.

The minister of education, Herbert Kirk, presented the recommendations of the Lockwood Committee to the cabinet in December 1964

Coleraine is located on the north coast of Northern Ireland, 90 km north-west of Belfast and 47 km north-east of Derry

Cabinet response to the Lockwood Report

The final two recommendations were by far the most controversial and the cabinet was particularly concerned about the proposal relating to Magee. After much discussion, Prime Minister Terence O'Neill insisted that the government response to the Lockwood Report would include the statement that 'the Government cannot agree that there is no alternative to the discontinuance of [Magee] College as a university institution'.[3]

Stormont Castle

The report was not published until February 1965, but rumours were already circulating in Derry about the recommendations of Lockwood in relation to Magee and the location of the second university. The strength of opposition to the report by the citizens of Derry was underestimated by O'Neill and his ministers. The controversy was to have a long-lasting impact on growing tensions between the nationalist community and the Stormont government.

REVIEW QUESTIONS

1	What were the consequences of the Education Act (1947) for education in Northern Ireland?
2	From an economic perspective, why would a second university benefit Northern Ireland?
3	Outline two reasons why many considered Derry as a suitable location for a university in the early 1960s.
4	What was the purpose of the Lockwood Committee?
5	Describe the membership of the Lockwood Committee.
6	What became evident to the Lockwood Committee by the time of their second meeting?
7	Why were Armagh and the 'new city' deemed unsuitable locations for a second university?
8	Referring to both the Coleraine and Derry proposals for a second university, explain why the Coleraine proposal was more attractive to the Lockwood Committee.
9	What aspect of the Lockwood Report was O'Neill's government most concerned about and how did they deal with this issue?

EXAMINE THE SOURCE

An edited extract from a proposal put forward by Derry Corporation on 1 January 1963 on why a second university for Northern Ireland should be located in the city of Derry.

1 The demand for university places in the 1970s may well be double the present one. It has been represented by a substantial body of responsible opinion that the establishment of a second university is the best way of meeting this demand.

2 It is a logical and obvious step to use Magee College as the nucleus [centre] round which to build a second independent university.

3 As a city, Derry is well situated geographically to support a university, and the establishment of a university in Derry would help to restore the equilibrium [balance] of Northern Ireland, educationally, economically and culturally. It is well served by communications with all parts of Northern Ireland and further afield.

4 Its modern growth as an industrial centre for the north-west, and as a military base, adds weight to its general claim for recognition as the most suitable locality for the establishment of a second university.

5 There are several highly suitable sites in the vicinity of Derry capable of housing a university.

6 Accommodation of students and staff presents no major problem.

7 The establishment of a university in Derry has aroused the support of all sections of its community.

8 The Council is prepared to sponsor a public foundation appeal and itself make an annual contribution equivalent to the product of a threepence rate towards the finances of the university for a period of ten years from the date of its foundation.

Source: Frank Curran, *Derry: Countdown to Disaster* (Dublin: Gill and Macmillan, 1986), pp. 27–29

1 According to point 1, why is a second university needed for Northern Ireland?
2 Why does the geographic position of Derry make it a suitable location for a university?
3 What is the Council prepared to do to contribute towards the financial costs of a second university?
4 Based on your reading of this document, what are the main strengths of the proposal put forward by Derry Corporation?
5 Based on your reading of this document, can you identify any weaknesses in the proposal?
6 Is this a useful historical source? Explain your answer.

The Coleraine University controversy (1965) and its impact

Guildhall, Derry

The University for Derry Committee was formed very quickly in response to rumours that the new university would be based in Coleraine. This chapter looks at the actions of this committee and the response of the government to them.

Useful terms

➤ **Cross-community** In Northern Ireland this refers to when both the Catholic and Protestant communities are involved in a particular event, issue or project.

➤ **Whip** This ensures that all members of a political party vote in line with party policy on important issues. A party official ('the whip') instructs members to vote in a particular way. Any party member who votes against the whip can be expelled from the party.

News that the Lockwood Committee had decided on Coleraine as a location for a second university prompted huge controversy in Derry. The University for Derry Committee quickly formed in response to the decision. They held a large protest meeting at the Guildhall in Derry and later organised a motorcade to Stormont, where representatives met with Terence O'Neill. However, the prime minister

In spite of campaigning from the University for Derry committee, Terence O'Neill remained firm in his resolve to accept the recommendations of the Lockwood report

remained firm in his resolve to accept the Lockwood recommendation. During a vote at Stormont he applied the whip to ensure that party members voted for the Coleraine proposal.

? KEY QUESTION

How did the Lockwood Report cause controversy in Derry and how did the people of Derry respond to it?

There was growing anger in Derry that the Lockwood report would not favour the city

What was the reaction to the Lockwood Report in Derry?

University for Derry Committee

Ahead of the publication of the Lockwood Report there was growing anger in Derry about rumours that the report recommendations would not favour the city. This led to the formation of a local action group, the **University for Derry Committee**, on 29 January 1965. A statement from the committee showed that it was not just the potential closure of Magee College that was a cause for concern but that there were wider problems at issue:

A railway signal cabin near Derry in 1959. By 1966, only one of the four original train lines into Derry remained in operation, contributing to a strong sense that the north-west region was being neglected.

There is growing feeling in Derry, even among Unionist supporters, that Government policy seems directed towards the isolation of the North-West in general and Derry in particular.
(*Derry Journal*, 29 January 1965)

The committee felt that a decision to locate a second university outside of their city was further evidence of government neglect of Derry, which had recently lost railway services and suffered from unemployment and lack of housing.

John Hume

The case for locating a university in Derry was supported by both the nationalist and unionist communities in the city. The University for Derry Committee consisted of three Catholic and three Protestant members. It was led by John Hume, a local Catholic teacher educated at Maynooth University, who had previously been involved in setting up a credit union movement in the city. His leadership of the action committee was his first involvement in a political campaign.

Public meeting at the Guildhall

A public meeting to support Derry's claim for a university was held at the Guildhall on 8 February 1965. It was organised by the University for Derry Committee and the Unionist mayor of the city, **Albert Anderson**. The Nationalist Party MP and leader of the opposition at Stormont, Eddie McAteer, was also on the platform at the meeting. Approximately 1,500 people were in attendance and the speakers emphasised the need for the whole community to unite on the issue. This was highlighted by Protestant city solicitor **Arthur Jack**, who stated that 'every citizen, irrespective of political view or religious persuasion, and every local organisation in this area stands solidly behind the city's claim'.[1]

Eddie McAteer, a Nationalist Party MP in the Stormont Parliament, was a leading figure in the 'University for Derry' campaign

Meeting with Terence O'Neill

The following day, Anderson, Hume and other members of the committee met with prime minister Terence O'Neill and minister of education **Herbert Kirk** at Stormont. They presented a resolution that had been passed at the public meeting, calling for the second university to be established in Derry. Hume told O'Neill that the committee was not prepared to accept any compromise on the issue and that the only solution was for a second university to be located in Derry.

Motorcade to Stormont

The committee wanted to make clear the strength and unity of the opposition to the Lockwood Report in Derry. To demonstrate this, a motorcade was organised to travel from Derry to Stormont on 18 February. Schools and businesses in the city closed in order to facilitate those attending the protest. Some of Derry's largest industrial employers, such as Monarch Electric, released workers to attend the motorcade. Those who could not travel to Stormont observed a two-minute silence at 3pm in Derry on the day of the motorcade.

The mayor was at the front of the motorcade and led a procession from the gates of Stormont up to the parliament buildings

It was estimated that 2,000 vehicles – including lorries, milk vans and cars – took part in the journey that started at the Guildhall in Derry and travelled through Strabane, Omagh and Dungannon before reaching Stormont, just outside Belfast. 'University for Derry' car stickers were distributed and no other emblems were allowed. This was part of the effort to show how all sides of the community were united on this issue.

The mayor, members of Derry Corporation and the University for Derry committee were at the front of the motorcade and led a procession from the gates of Stormont up to the parliament buildings. Cars lined the driveway and an overflow of vehicles spread out into the avenues and roads surrounding Stormont. The official delegation from Derry presented a petition to O'Neill and gave him maps of sites in Derry where a university could be located. O'Neill's response was lukewarm, however, and Anderson told journalists that 'the Prime Minister did not commit himself in any way' when presented with the documents.[2]

What was Stormont's response to the Lockwood Report?

The Unionist government at Stormont was somewhat taken aback

? KEY QUESTION
How did O'Neill ensure that the Lockwood recommendations were accepted by the Stormont parliament?

by the strength of opposition to the Lockwood Report in Derry. However, in the parliamentary debates that followed O'Neill undertook measures to ensure that the Lockwood recommendations were accepted.

Meeting with the 'faceless men'

The day after the Stormont motorcade, Terence O'Neill held a secret meeting with seven high-profile members of the Ulster Unionist Party from Derry. It was not widely known that this meeting had taken

The 'faceless men' had been trying to ensure that Magee College would form some part of the new university

place until May 1965, when Unionist MP Robert Nixon referred in a speech to '**nameless, faceless men**' who had tried to influence O'Neill in relation to the university controversy.

At the time, Nixon alleged that the unionists had tried to persuade O'Neill to ignore the plea from Derry and to locate the university in Coleraine. However, the minutes of the meeting later revealed that in fact the 'faceless men' were trying to ensure that Magee College would form some part of the new university. Nonetheless, sectarian attitudes were clearly evident during the discussion. Both O'Neill and the unionist men revealed their concerns that the economic development of Derry might lead to a further increase in the Catholic population, which would threaten the political control that unionists held in the city. Unionist control of the city was based on a delicate system of **gerrymandering** (see p. 9 and p. 17) and changes in the balance of the population would lead to unionists losing their majority hold on Derry Corporation.

Stormont debate

The debate in the Stormont parliament on the Lockwood Report lasted 16 hours and took place over three days in March 1965. The debate was at times heated and O'Neill rejected allegations that the decision to locate the university in Coleraine was evidence of discrimination against the city of Derry. O'Neill decided to apply the **whip** in a vote to approve the Lockwood Report. This meant that Ulster Unionist Party members were instructed to vote in favour of the motion and if they failed to do so they would be expelled from the party. The vote was carried by 27 votes to 19. Two members of the Ulster Unionist Party voted against the motion and one abstained.

Nixon allegations

The vote in Stormont ended all hopes in Derry that a second university would be located in their city. The controversy was reignited two months later when Robert Nixon referred to the meeting with the 'faceless men' (see previous page) in a speech in Derry. Nixon's allegations did little to quell nationalist suspicions that the Lockwood Report was a unionist conspiracy to deny a second university to the majority Catholic city of Derry.

Not only did Nixon allege that the men had tried to influence O'Neill to favour the Coleraine proposal, he also made the accusation that John Lockwood had been directed by a government minister to locate the university at Coleraine. Nixon was expelled from the party shortly after his speech. A petition calling for an inquiry into the proceedings of the Lockwood Committee was signed by 15,000 people but was ignored by the government.

Lockwood made a statement denying this accusation. The release of **archival material** relating to the proceedings of the Lockwood Committee thirty years later did show that senior civil servants in Stormont worked closely with the committee and had some influence over them. However, a historian who closely examined this material concluded that: 'the Lockwood Committee made its decision on the location of the university on the basis of practices long accepted as sound with regard to the establishment of new British universities'.[3]

What is clearly evident is that the Lockwood Committee did not grasp the particular situation of Northern Ireland. It underestimated how its decision to locate the university in Coleraine would ignite the already simmering tensions over the perceived neglect of the Catholic majority north-west of the province.

What was the impact of the Coleraine University controversy?

The Coleraine University controversy contributed to a growing sense of injustice among the nationalist community in Northern Ireland. Rightly or wrongly, many Catholics believed that the decision to locate the new university at Coleraine was a deliberate decision by the unionist government to isolate Derry. The university issue, combined with other grievances on issues relating to housing, employment and voting rights led to the beginning of the civil rights movement in 1968.

John Hume's first involvement in political activism was the University for Derry campaign. He went on to play a key role in the civil rights movement and in nationalist politics up until the early 2000s

The controversy was a political awakening for many of those who were involved with the University for Derry Committee. Members such as John Hume went on to become activists in the civil rights movement marches that began three years later, in 1968. Hume later said of the controversy: 'The university decision ... electrified the people on the nationalist side, and I think was really the spark that ignited the civil rights movement.'[4]

The controversy over the location of a second university in Coleraine contributed to a growing sense of grievance that gave rise to the civil rights movement that began in 1968

The controversy badly damaged the new cross-community alliances that had been developing under Terence O'Neill (see p. 16). O'Neill had developed a reputation as a leader that had the ability to reach out to the nationalist community; however, his handling of the Coleraine University controversy damaged this image.

REVIEW QUESTIONS

1	Apart from the university issue, in what ways did the University for Derry Committee feel that Derry was suffering neglect by 1965?
2	Who was John Hume and why was his involvement with the University for Derry Committee significant?
3	Based on the meeting at the Guildhall, what evidence is there that the campaign for a university for Derry was a cross-community one?
4	How did the University for Derry Committee demonstrate the strength and unity of the opposition in Derry to the decision of the Lockwood Committee?
5	What was the motorcade to Stormont?

6	How did O'Neill respond to the petition presented to him by representatives of the motorcade?
7	Who were the 'nameless, faceless men' who met with O'Neill on 19 February 1965?
8	What sectarian attitudes were revealed in the discussion between O'Neill and the 'faceless men'?
9	Explain your understanding of the term 'apply the whip' as it related to the vote on the Lockwood Report in the Stormont parliament.
10	What was the impact of Robert Nixon's allegations on the nationalist community in Derry?
11	Based on the evidence you have read in this book, do you think the decision of the Lockwood Committee in relation to a university at Coleraine was a fair one? Explain your answer.
12	Describe and discuss two major impacts of the Coleraine University controversy.

EXAMINE THE SOURCES

Source 1

Coleraine

It is only four miles from Coleraine to the seaside resorts of Portrush and Portstewart. The three towns form a triangle of rich bogland. Somewhere here, a new university is expected to rise up from the brown earth within the next two or three years, eventually catering for a student population of 7,000.

Northern Ireland should have a second university and this is the best location for it – that is the view of Sir John Lockwood's committee on adult education ... The news has delighted the Coleraine district and incensed Derry, the other principal contender for the university ...

The impartial layman might ask why Coleraine was chosen in preference to Derry city, which already has Magee University College, or Armagh, with its long ecclesiastical tradition. Coleraine, many say, is just another Northern provincial town with none of the historical or academic significance of Derry or Armagh ...

The town has a tidy, Presbyterian appearance – the population is 13,000, over 70% of which is Protestant ...

There is little unemployment. There are four important industries in the town, including the American Chemstrand factory, where synthetic man-made fibre is manufactured. Coleraine also is a port and an administrative centre for Co. Derry ...

Portrush and Portstewart, the other towns of the triangle, play a dormitory role to Coleraine. As seaside resorts their traditional reliance is on the few months of a northern tourist season. In contrast to Coleraine, there is an air of depression and desertion in the resorts after September ...

But this picture of depression may soon change for the boarding-houses and cafés of these two resorts. With the new university only a few miles away, the reliance on the short tourist season is likely to be supplanted [replaced] by the accommodation requirements of the new student population, which is expected to number at least 2,000 by 1968.

Source: Andrew Hamilton, 'Northern Town on Road to Prosperity', *The Irish Times*, 15 February 1965

(a) What size student population is the new university expected to cater for?
(b) According to the article, why is it surprising that Coleraine has been chosen as the location for a second university for Northern Ireland?
(c) What percentage of the population of the town is Protestant?
(d) What evidence is there in this article that Coleraine is a prosperous town?
(e) How is the location of the university in Coleraine expected to benefit the towns of Portrush and Portstewart?

Source 2

Motorcade to Stormont

A crowd of several thousands pack Guildhall Square and as the official cars containing the members of the corporation and members of the University for Derry Committee moved off they were cheered on their way ...

About 200 vehicles left the Guildhall starting point and they drove along the streets lined with people to Craigavon Bridge. Traffic lights on the way were switched off and police on duty at Foyle Street and the end of the bridge ensured that the vast cavalcade got away to a very smooth and easy start ...

All types of vehicles were there to give the procession a really representative appearance. There were the limousines of the corporation, followed by heavy lorries, milk vans, petrol lorries, break-down vans and cars of every make and size.

On the way through the city girls wearing "University for Derry" streamers as head-coverings and waving red and white coloured scarves, greeted the cavalcade.

The city itself had a holiday atmosphere, with shops, schools and public houses closed.

A two minute silence was observed in the city. Most traffic stopped and pedestrians stood bare-headed as the Guildhall struck three.

Source: 'Motorcade got an Enthusiastic Send-off', *Derry Journal*, 19 February 1965

(a) Who travelled in the official cars that departed the Guildhall?

(b) How many vehicles left the Guildhall?

(c) What type of vehicles took part in the motorcade?

(d) What was observed at 3pm?

(e) Identify at least two pieces of evidence to show that there was widespread support for the motorcade in the city of Derry.

(f) From your knowledge of the Coleraine University controversy, was the motorcade to Stormont an effective protest?

Source 3

John Hume on the Coleraine University controversy

Our [the people of Derry's] growing sense of isolation was enhanced by the closure of our rail links to Donegal in 1953 and to Dublin in 1965, and the subsequent downgrading of the link to Belfast. When Prime Minister O'Neill embarked on a modernisation campaign in 1963, he focused on the area to the east of the River Bann, overlooking Derry and its environs. The final straw was the recommendation, in 1965, that a new university be constructed in the small neighbouring town of Coleraine, rather than in the city of Derry, which already had the historic buildings of Magee College, the obvious site for a new seat of learning. All of these grievances produced an inevitable momentum, which led to the dynamic and widely supported civil rights campaign ...

These were the conditions that led me into public life. I had been one of the lucky ones: I was the first of my generation to take advantage of the 1947 Education Act and get myself to university. My education allowed me to put something back into my community. I became involved in housing and poverty and self-help organisations. Along with others, I helped establish the Derry Credit Union movement – the first in Northern Ireland – in 1960, and the Derry Housing Association in 1965 ...

I became chairman of the University for Derry campaign when both traditions in the city united in protest against the decision to site the new university in Coleraine. It was a battle we'd lost before we began, but it was still significant, showing us the potential for moving forward through non-violent direct action.

Source: John Hume, 'Transforming the Union: an evolving dynamic' in *Britain and Ireland: Lives Entwined III* (British Council Ireland, 2008)

(a) Give three reasons why John Hume felt that the city of Derry was being isolated by the Stormont government in the 1960s.

(b) Why did John Hume consider himself 'one of the lucky ones'?

(c) Why, according to John Hume, was the University for Derry campaign significant?

(d) This account was written by John Hume approximately forty years after the Coleraine University controversy. How does this impact on the value of this account as a source for historians?

DOCUMENTS-BASED QUESTIONS

The following are two documents-based questions. Use them to practise for your exam.

Question 1 (Higher Level)

Study the two sources below and answer the questions that follow.

Document A

An edited extract from a speech by Herbert Kirk, minister of education. Kirk describes the criteria used by the Lockwood Committee to decide on a location for a second university in a speech at Stormont, 3 March 1965.

The principal criteria are:

(a) There must be an adequate and suitable site of at least 300 acres.

(b) The location must be one in which development can proceed smoothly and successfully. Here the [Lockwood] Committee add that a particular location should not be chosen chiefly for the good it may do to the location chosen.

(c) The chosen area must be attractive to academic staff and to their families and must rank high in the amenities which it can offer.

(d) Lodgings must be available in appreciable [sufficient] numbers as financial and material resources must initially be concentrated on academic building.

(e) There must be an adequate supporting population within reasonable travelling distance to service the new university.

(f) The location must have good communications with other parts of Northern Ireland and with Great Britain, but it must also be sufficiently away from the pull of Belfast to ensure that the character and background of the new university will make it different from Queen's University ...

The Committee also says that it is impossible to give a precise weighting to each relevant factor, but that in its concerted view the Coleraine area satisfies its criteria better than any of the other areas considered and that in its opinion the new university will have the best opportunity of a good start and of ultimate success in that area.

Source: Public Records Office of Northern Ireland, CAB/9/D/31/2

Document B

An edited extract from an open memorandum from Derry Corporation to the members of the Stormont parliament, entitled 'The Criteria that Count', 26 February 1965.

These are the questions which [the Lockwood Committee] have asked about the location of the new university. These, it is suggested, are the questions which you also must ask:

Is it not right that a university in which prominence is to be given to the biological sciences ... and to agriculture, should be located in the area which can offer the greatest variety of natural resources for study and research in these subjects?

Is it not right that a university which is also to be a centre of teacher education, should be located in the area which can provide within easy reach the greatest variety of educational institutions?

Is it not right that a university which is to counteract the attraction now exercised by the concentration of higher education facilities in Belfast, should be located in or immediately adjacent to the only major centre of population in the Province beyond the periphery of greater Belfast?

Are not these considerations of far more importance than the availability of boarding-houses and hotels throughout the winter months for short-term student accommodation ...? And is there not only one location which satisfies all these requirements – Londonderry, which in Magee University College already possesses all the accommodation, teaching, administrative, and lodging, necessary to serve as a ready-made spring-board to the new university?

Source: Public Records Office of Northern Ireland, CAB/9/D/31/2

1 Comprehension

(a) According to document A, what was the requirement of the Lockwood Committee in relation to lodgings (accommodation)?
(b) According to document A, what reasons were given as to why Coleraine was chosen as a location for a second university?
(c) According to document B, what is important to have located near a centre of teacher education?
(d) Why, according to document B, does Londonderry satisfy the requirements for the location of a university?

2 Comparison

(a) Document A shows that the Lockwood Committee found that Coleraine was the most suitable location for a university. How do the points put forward in document B contradict this finding?
(b) In your opinion, which document makes the stronger argument for where a second university should be located? Support your answer with evidence from both documents.

3 Criticism

(a) According to document A, a university location should not 'be chosen chiefly for the good it may do to the location chosen'. Explain your understanding of this point. How does it relate to the debate over choosing a location for the university?

(b) Do you consider document B to be an objective source? Explain your answer.

4 Contextualisation

To what extent did the decision to locate a second university in Coleraine show evidence of the deliberate neglect of the city of Derry by the unionist government of Terence O'Neill?

Question 2 (Ordinary Level)

Study the two sources below and answer the questions that follow.

Document A

Notice advertising a public meeting in Derry, 8 February 1965.

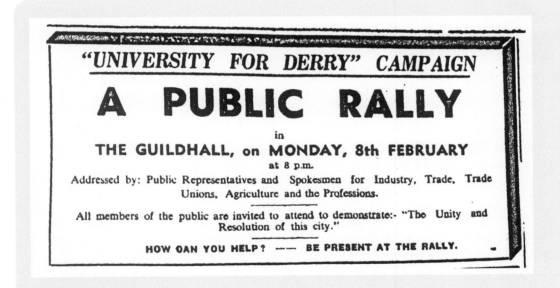

Source: Derry Journal, 5 February 1965

Document B

Newspaper report on a meeting that took place at the Guildhall in Derry, 8 February 1965.

The meeting, which was attended by upwards of 1,500 people, was one of the largest seen in the city in recent years and was easily the most representative gathering to assemble in the city for a considerable time.

Amongst the speakers were Mr. Eddie McAteer. M.P. Mr. P Gormley. M.P. Miss Sheelagh Murnaghan. M.P. Mr. D. Bleakley, the Labour Party spokesman on education.

Mr. John Hume, acting chairman of the committee, who presided at the meeting, said that the purpose of the meeting was to show that the people of Derry not only claimed the second university but expected it to be established in the city. "We must show that we feel about this matter," he said.

Source: Derry Journal, 9 February 1965

1 Comprehension

(a) According to document A, what organisation is hosting the public rally at the Guildhall?
(b) According to document A, who is invited to attend the meeting at the Guildhall?
(c) How many people attended the rally, according to document B?
(d) What, according to document B, was the role of John Hume during the meeting?

2 Comparison

(a) In document A the organisers called on the public to 'be present at the rally'. Based on the evidence in document B, were the organisers successful in achieving this aim?
(b) Which source is more useful to a historian, document A or document B? Give reasons for your answer.

3 Criticism

(a) Say whether each of these sources is a primary or secondary source. Give reasons for your choice in each case.
(b) In document B, what do you think John Hume meant when he told the crowd, 'we must show that we feel about this matter'?

4 Contextualisation

Why did the decision to establish a university at Coleraine provoke controversy?

Question 3 (Higher Level)

Study the two sources below and answer the questions that follow.

Document A

An edited extract from a private letter from Roy Henderson, an Ulster Unionist Party councillor on Derry Corporation, to Prime Minister Terence O'Neill, 25 February 1965.

You will be aware that since your recent discussions with the Prime Minister of the Republic political tensions in Londonderry have eased very considerably. I form the impression that local members of the Nationalist Party are going to great lengths to encourage this easing of tensions. It may be that they are doing so because they sincerely believe such a course to be in the best interests of this City. They may on the other hand have completely different reasons – who knows? However, whatever the reasons may be, the fact is that the Nationalists in Londonderry – particularly those who are members of the Corporation – appear to have joined whole-heartedly with the Unionists in presenting a united City and a united claim for the establishment of a University in Londonderry. If the claim is successful much good may ensue locally not only socially, economically and culturally but also perhaps politically. If on the other hand the claim fails I foresee very great difficulties for Londonderry – difficulties which are bound to have repercussions throughout the Province.

Source: Public Records Office of Northern Ireland, CAB/9/D/31/2

Document B

An edited extract from a speech by John Hume at a public meeting of the Campaign for Democracy in Ulster, Fulham Town Hall, July 1965.

Not a single academic criterion is to be found in the [Lockwood] Report for the choice of Coleraine [...] The plan is therefore to develop the strongly unionist Belfast-Portadown-Coleraine triangle and to cause a migration from west to east Ulster, redistributing and scattering the minority so that the Unionist Party will not only maintain but strengthen its position. The British taxpayer is paying for these schemes. The new university will cost over £200 million. Yet it would appear that the Treasury doles out this size of capital [finance] without attempting to scrutinize in any detail the uses to which it will be put. The tragedy is that this plan comes at a time when the Northern Ireland problem shows more hopeful signs of [an] internal solution than ever before. [...] There has been a great growth in liberal feeling, but unfortunately, it is my fear that by the time this upsurge in tolerance and right thinking reaches the corridors of power in Northern Ireland, it will be too late for places like Derry, and irreparable damage will have been done. The unionist administration must be taught that they cannot run away from Derry and West Ulster, and that if they seriously want to create a modern community they must treat all citizens with dignity and equality.

Source: Seán Farren (ed.), *John Hume: In His Own Words* (Dublin: Four Courts Press, 2018), pp. 27–28

1 Comprehension

(a) According to document A, what has caused tensions in Londonderry to ease considerably?

(b) According to document A, if the claim for a university in Londonderry is successful, what impact will this have?

(c) In document B, who does John Hume say will pay for the new university and how much will it cost?

(d) According to document A, how can the unionist administration create a modern community in Northern Ireland?

2 Comparison

(a) Is document B in agreement with document A that tensions between nationalists and unionists have eased in recent times? Give reasons for your answer, referring to both documents.

(b) Do both documents agree that failing to locate a second university in Derry will have an impact on the relationship between nationalists and unionists in Northern Ireland as a whole? Give reasons for your answer, referring to both documents.

3 Criticism

(a) What are the strengths and weaknesses of document A as a historical source?

(b) Based on your knowledge of the period and the evidence in document B, why, do you think, did John Hume believe that the decision to locate the university in Coleraine was driven by a Unionist Party political agenda?

4 Contextualisation

What was the impact of the Coleraine University controversy on relations between nationalists and unionists in Northern Ireland?

CASE STUDY B:

The Apprentice Boys of Derry

5 The origins of the Apprentice Boys of Derry organisation

The siege of Derry, 17th century

The Apprentice Boys of Derry was founded in 1813 to commemorate a historic event, the siege of Derry, 1688–1689. Annual commemorations continue to take place in the city. Participation in parades and events organised by the Apprentice Boys is viewed as an important expression of Protestant cultural identity.

Useful terms

» **Commemoration** This is a way of remembering events from the past. Commemoration usually involves the participation of members of the public and can take different forms, for example a memorial plaque or monument, a formal ceremony, a parade, etc.

» **Depose** To remove someone from office by force, such as overthrowing a king or queen.

» **Effigy** A three-dimensional representation of a person. An effigy can sometimes take the form of a caricature of the person and is often burned.

» **Ritual** In the case of the Apprentice Boys of Derry, a ritual is an action that took place at a specific time and place to commemorate the events of the siege of Derry.

» **Siege** A military operation in which enemy forces surround a town, cutting off essential supplies.

The **siege of Derry, 1688–1689** is seen as a key event of the **Williamite-Jacobite War** in Ireland between the forces of the deposed Catholic king **James II** and his Protestant son-in-law **William of Orange**. James II was the Catholic king of England, Scotland and Ireland from 1685

> **? KEY QUESTION**
> What was the siege of Derry (1688–1689) and how did it lead to the formation of the Apprentice Boys of Derry?

to 1688. During the **Glorious Revolution**, his Protestant daughter Mary and her Dutch husband, William of Orange, overthrew James with the aim of restoring Protestant rule to the three kingdoms.

James II

William of Orange

James II looked for support in Ireland, where there was a majority Catholic population. However, there was a substantial number of Protestants living in Ireland and they were concentrated in areas such as **Derry**, where the population were supporters of William and Mary. The town had been renamed **Londonderry** during the Ulster Plantation in the early 17th century when a large number of tradespeople had emigrated from London to settle there.

A contemporary illustration of the siege of Derry in 1689

Taking control of Derry was seen as a necessary move by James II in order to assert Catholic control of Ireland and threaten the power of William and Mary in England. In December 1689, James II ordered the Catholic Earl of Tyrconnell to install his forces in the city of Derry.

What were the key events of the siege of Derry?

A number of important events took place during the siege of Derry. These events are significant because they later formed the basis of commemorative events organised by the Apprentice Boys of Derry.

1. **Shutting of the gates**: The shutting of the gates occurred on 7 December 1688. On seeing the approaching forces of the **Earl of Tyrconnell**, a group of thirteen **apprentice boys** rushed to shut the gates of the walled city and prevented the forces from entering.

2. **Treachery of Lundy**: In April 1689, James II and his forces arrived outside Derry to take the city. The governor of Derry at the time was **Robert Lundy**. Lundy is believed to have hesitated on how to respond to this development and advised that the citizens of Derry negotiate an agreement with James. The citizens were against this proposal and Lundy was forced to escape the city disguised as a soldier. Two co-governors, **Reverend George Walker** and **Major Henry Baker** took over the running of the city.

3. **Relief of Derry**: The siege of Derry lasted for 105 days. A boom was constructed by the besieging forces across the **River Foyle**, preventing supplies from getting to the inhabitants. It is estimated that 10,000 citizens died during the siege, mostly from hunger and disease. On 12 August 1689 the relief of Derry occurred when *Mountjoy*, a merchant ship, broke through the boom and, with another ship, unloaded many tons of food in the city. This development prompted the forces laying siege to the city to decamp, bringing the siege to an end.

REV. GEORGE WALKER
From an engraving of the portrait by Sir Godfrey Kneller

George Walker, one of two governors of Derry during the siege of Derry

The following year, in July 1690 the Jacobite-Williamite War was brought to a definitive end when the forces of William of Orange defeated the forces of James II in the **battle of the Boyne**.

William of Orange leading his army to victory over James II in the battle of the Boyne on 12 July 1690

What was the significance of the siege?

Both the siege of Derry and the battle of the Boyne have become symbolic events in the Protestant tradition in Northern Ireland. Annual commemorations of these events are seen as important expressions of Protestant identity. The battle of the Boyne is commemorated annually on 12 July by the **Orange Order** (see p. 3). It is viewed as a symbol of Protestant victory over Catholics in Ireland.

The focus of this case study is the commemoration of the siege of Derry. These commemorations are organised by the **Apprentice Boys of Derry**. The siege is an important symbol of Protestant resistance against Catholic oppression. The 'No surrender!' rallying cry of those under siege in Derry became a popular slogan in Protestant culture. The struggle of the citizens of Derry in 1689 is also seen to reflect how the Protestant minority on the island of Ireland has sometimes felt under siege from the majority Catholic population.

An illustration of the apprentices shutting the gates in 1688

The Apprentice Boys of Derry Memorial Hall, which is now a museum of the siege of Derry

Commemoration of the siege, 1689–1949

In the century after it occurred, the events of the siege of Derry were commemorated by its citizens. At first, commemorations occurred sporadically, but over time they became more formal and different **rituals** developed around commemorating the events of 1688–1689.

The annual ceremony of the burning of an effigy of Robert Lundy continues up until the present day

In the 1770s, two commemorative events developed which survived into the 20th century and beyond. The first event was the commemoration of the 'shutting of the gates' which was marked in and around 7 December each year. From 1788 onwards, an **effigy** of the traitor Robert Lundy was burned and those participating wore orange ribbons to represent the Protestant tradition established by William of Orange. The second event occurred in August of each year, when groups would commemorate the relief of Derry, sometimes by carrying out re-enactments of the siege itself.

Foundation of the Apprentice Boys

The first **Apprentice Boys of Derry Club** was formed in Dublin in 1813. However, this group did not participate in commemorative events in Derry. In October 1824 the **No Surrender Club of the Apprentice Boys** was founded in Derry and immediately took over the organisation of siege commemorations. Other similar clubs were established in the city in the following years.

Nineteenth-century illustration of the Walker Monument in Derry

The 'Roaring Meg' cannon from the siege of Derry that overlooks the Catholic Bogside area of the city

The establishment of Apprentice Boys clubs led to new commemorative practices that became part of Apprentice Boys tradition. Club members rescued a sunken cannon used in the siege of Derry called the **Roaring Meg** from the River Foyle and installed it in the city walls. Firing of cannons became part of the annual August commemorations of the siege. The clubs also raised money for a statue of **George Walker**, the governor of Derry during the siege. The **Walker Testimonial** was placed on the Royal Bastion of the city walls, directly overlooking the **Bogside area** of the city, where the Catholic population lived. The burning of the Lundy effigy now took place at the Walker Testimonial in December. In August, the Apprentice Boys included a procession past the Walker statue as part of their parade.

The historian Heather Stanfiel has noted that the location of the Walker Testimonial 'directly over Catholic houses served to increase tension as the monument immediately became the most visible symbol of loyalist sentiment in Derry'.[1] In the 19th century, the Catholic population of Derry was on the increase and by 1851 there was a majority of Catholics living in the city. The positioning of the Walker Testimonial in such a prominent position helped to assert Protestant authority in Derry.

The Apprentice Boys prior to 1949

Membership of the Apprentice Boys clubs increased rapidly from the 1880s onwards. In 1889 the general committee of the Apprentice Boys permitted clubs to be established outside the walls of Derry, which led to a growth in membership of the organisation.

The growth of the Apprentice Boys has also been linked to political events. The growth in support for home rule in Ireland in the late 19th century (see p. 2) led to an increase in the numbers joining the Apprentice Boys organisation. The Protestant community in Ulster felt threatened by home rule and they joined the Apprentice Boys as they saw the organisation as supporting the Protestant, unionist tradition. Similarly, when Ireland was **partitioned** in 1921 (see p. 5) Protestants in Derry felt under threat. Their city was located near the border between the newly created states of Northern Ireland and the Irish Free State and many Protestants continued to join the Apprentice Boys as a way of expressing their cultural identity.

Portrait of a member of the Apprentice Boys in 1917

REVIEW QUESTIONS

1	The Jacobite-Williamite war involved which two kings?
2	What happened during the Glorious Revolution?
3	Why did James II want to take control of Derry?
4	What was the 'shutting of the gates' that occurred in December 1689?
5	Who was Robert Lundy and how did he become known as a traitor?
6	What happened on 12 August 1689?
7	From the 1770s onwards, how were the events of December 1689 commemorated in Derry?
8	Describe the foundation of the Apprentice Boys organisation in the 1800s.

9	What was controversial about the location of the Walker Testimonial?
10	What political events led to an increase in the membership of the Apprentice Boys?
11	Why did these political events lead to an increase in the membership of the Apprentice Boys?

EXAMINE THE SOURCE

A crowd watches the burning of the effigy of Lundy in Derry on 13 December 1968
(*Londonderry Sentinel*, 18 December 1967)

(a) Describe the scene in the photograph.

(b) Based on your knowledge of the Apprentice Boys of Derry, where was the burning of the effigy of Lundy traditionally carried out?

(c) Based on the evidence in the photo, would you agree that this ceremony was viewed as intimidating by some citizens in Derry? Explain your answer.

6 The Apprentice Boys of Derry, 1949–1993

Two youths during the battle of the Bogside

By 1949 the Apprentice Boys of Derry was a large organisation and thousands of members participated in its annual commemorations of the siege of Derry. Membership of the Apprentice Boys became an expression of Protestant cultural identity. However, their activities were sometimes seen by the Catholic community as intimidating and representing Protestant dominance and control of Derry. The organisation was associated with key events in the outbreak of the Troubles.

Useful terms

➤ **Royal Ulster Constabulary (RUC)** This was the police force of Northern Ireland, formed in 1922. Membership of the police force was mostly Protestant.

By the 1950s the Apprentice Boys of Derry was a well-established organisation, with branches located as far afield as Scotland and Canada. Every December, the Apprentice Boys re-enacted the shutting of the gates that marked the beginning of the city's resistance against the forces of James II and burned an effigy of the traitor Lundy at the Walker monument. In August, a

> **? KEY QUESTION**
> How did the Apprentice Boys of Derry function as an expression of Protestant identity and how did this impact on Catholics in Derry?

Mural depicting the shutting of the gates during the siege of Derry, located in the Protestant Waterside area of the city. Commemorating the events of the siege continues to be an important expression of Protestant cultural identity

procession took place along the city walls to celebrate the relief of the city. In the 1950s, between 5,000 and 8,000 Apprentice Boys took part in the parade each year.

The development of the civil rights movement in the 1960s brought the Apprentice Boys into conflict with the Catholic community. The organisation was associated with key events in the outbreak of the Troubles: the civil rights march on 5 October 1968 and the battle of the Bogside in August 1969.

How was the Apprentice Boys an expression of Protestant cultural identity?

As a result of its commemoration of the siege of Derry and its long history as an organisation with Protestant membership, by 1949 the Apprentice Boys of Derry had come to represent different aspects of Protestant cultural identity in Northern Ireland:

» **The history of the Protestant community in Ulster:** The main purpose of the Apprentice Boys was to commemorate the siege of Derry 1688–1689, where the Protestant citizens of Derry triumphed over their Catholic enemies and successfully overturned the siege.

» **Protestant authority:** The Apprentice Boys functioned as a symbol of the power of the Protestant community in Northern Ireland. The need to assert this authority was particularly strong in Derry, where there was a majority Catholic population. The Apprentice Boys' annual parade along the walls of the city that overlooked the Catholic Bogside was a practice that asserted Protestant control of the city.

» **Symbol of resistance:** Members of the Apprentice Boys sometimes likened their situation to that of the citizens of Derry in 1689. They too felt under siege from Catholics, many of whom desired a united Ireland while the Apprentice Boys wanted Northern Ireland to remain a part of the United Kingdom. Like the citizens of 1689, the Apprentice Boys were determined not to surrender power to Catholics.

What was the impact of the Apprentice Boys on the Catholic community?

For the Catholic community in Derry, the existence of the Apprentice Boys and their annual commemorations served as an unwelcome reminder of Protestant control of the city. By the 1950s and 1960s, a system of **gerrymandering** was well established in Derry (see also p. 9 and p. 17). This was where the boundaries of electoral wards were manipulated to ensure that the Ulster Unionist Party held a majority of seats on Derry Corporation, even though the majority of the electorate was Catholic. The annual commemoration ceremonies of the Apprentice Boys added to the growing resentment among the Catholic community of Protestant dominance in the city.

The Catholic community also found the activities of the Apprentice Boys intimidating. Not only did the marches take place overlooking the Bogside, but a custom developed where Apprentice Boys would throw coins down on the Bogside. Overall, the provocative activities of the Apprentice Boys was one of a number of grievances felt by the Catholic community that eventually led to the development of the **civil rights movement** in the late 1960s (see p. 16).

Did the Apprentice Boys contribute to the outbreak of the Troubles?

Civil rights march in Derry, 5 October 1968

The civil rights movement emerged in Northern Ireland with the formation of groups such as the **Northern Ireland Civil Rights Association** (NICRA) and the **Derry Housing Action Committee** in 1967. These organisations were mostly made up of young Catholic activists who sought to use peaceful protest in order to campaign on issues such as voting rights and the allocation of housing.

? KEY QUESTION
Did the activities of the Apprentice Boys of Derry contribute to the outbreak of the Troubles in 1968 and 1969?

The civil rights movement gained momentum throughout 1968. Following the success of a protest march in Co. Tyrone in August, when 2,500 people marched from **Coalisland to Dungannon** to protest against discrimination in the allocation of housing, another protest march was planned to take place in Derry on 5 October 1968.

A confrontation between members of the RUC and a civil rights protestor during the march in Derry, 5 October 1968

William Craig, minister of home affairs in 1968

Members of NICRA decided that the march would follow 'a traditional Protestant route from the Waterside on the east of the Foyle, over Craigavon Bridge to the Diamond in the heart of the walled city'.[1] Five days before the march was due to take place, the Apprentice Boys of Derry announced that they would be holding a procession on the same day, following the same route as the NICRA protest. Given that Apprentice Boys events took place only in August and December, the decision to hold a parade in October was seen as a deliberate attempt by the Apprentice Boys to disrupt the NICRA protest.

On 3 October, **William Craig**, the minister of home affairs, banned any marches from taking place in Derry. The Apprentice Boys cancelled their procession but the civil rights campaigners decided to go ahead with their protest. The march ended with violent clashes between protestors and police, film footage of which was broadcast around the world. The incident sparked widespread outrage that the **RUC** police force would baton-charge a group of unarmed protestors.

Battle of the Bogside, August 1969

The Apprentice Boys parade in Derry on 12 August 1969 was the event that sparked the **battle of the Bogside**, considered the first major event of the Troubles. Tensions had been building across Northern Ireland since the October 1968 march. This was particularly the case in Derry, where rioting had broken out in April after the government banned a civil rights march in the city.

John Hume addresses members of the Catholic community in Celtic football ground on 10 August 1969 as tension built before the Apprentice Boys parade

The parade was anticipated for some time as a potential flashpoint for violence between the nationalist community and the RUC police force. Prior to the march, residents of the Bogside prepared for violence by making petrol bombs and other homemade weapons. Leading members of the civil rights movement, such as **John Hume** and **Ivan Cooper**, appealed to the Catholic community for restraint. They also held talks with high-ranking members of the Apprentice Boys in an effort to persuade them to call off the parade. However, the Apprentice Boys 'insisted on the right of unionists to march in any part of Northern Ireland at any time'.[2] The government, under new prime minister James Chichester-Clark, considered calling off the march but eventually allowed it to proceed.

On the afternoon of 12 August, the Apprentice Boys parade passed through **Waterloo Place**, a small square in the centre of Derry. Nationalist supporters began jeering the marchers and singing songs in an effort to drown out the marching tunes played by the Apprentice Boys. Some of the nationalists began to throw stones at police gathered in the square and those marching in the procession. In spite of this, the Apprentice Boys kept marching and playing their instruments.

Violence intensified between nationalists and the RUC in the William Street area and quickly descended into full-scale rioting. The Apprentice Boys were not involved in this violence and the thousands of marchers in the parade had disappeared from the city by the end of the day. The rioting continued and was brought to an end only when the British Army arrived on the streets of Derry at 5pm on 14 August.

Images showing the Apprentice Boys parade as it passed through the streets of Derry on 12 August 1969

Young people making petrol bombs during the battle of the Bogside

What were the activities of the Apprentice Boys during the Troubles?

Following the violence of August 1969, both of the annual marches of the Apprentice Boys were banned for the next two years. Marches were held between 1972 and 1974 but on a much smaller scale than previously. They were confined to the Protestant **Waterside area** on the east bank of the River Foyle.

Bombing of the Walker Testimonial

In August 1973 the Walker Testimonial was bombed by the IRA. The monument had not formed part of Apprentice Boys' commemorations since the banning of marches but it continued to be viewed by the nationalist community as a symbol of unionist dominance in Derry. The custom of burning the effigy of Lundy every December eventually moved to **Bishop's Gate** in the city.

Tercentenary commemoration of the siege of Derry

From 1975, the Apprentice Boys were allowed to march in a small area within the walled city. In 1989, commemorations of the **tercentenary** (three-hundred year) anniversary of the siege of Derry was organised by **Derry City Council** in co-operation with the Apprentice Boys. The council was now under the majority control of nationalist politicians. Efforts were made to make commemorations of the siege more inclusive by emphasising that the historic event was part of a shared history of both the Protestant and Catholic communities in Derry.

Scenes of rioting on the streets of Derry that occurred in the days following the Apprentice Boys parade

The Walker Testimonial after the bombing by the IRA in 1973

It was not until 1995 that they were once again permitted to parade along the city walls and provocative customs such as the throwing of coins towards the Bogside have been removed.

Growth of the Apprentice Boys during the Troubles

The number of Apprentice Boys clubs and their membership increased throughout the Troubles. In 1971 there were 178 Apprentice Boys clubs and by 1989 that number had grown to over 200. The growth in numbers joining Apprentice Boys clubs and an increase in the

An Apprentice Boys parade in Derry in 1978. In spite of restrictions, Apprentice Boys events continued to take place throughout the era of the Troubles

frequency of parades has been attributed to the wider feeling among the unionist community of being under threat from the nationalist community since the outbreak of the Troubles. As the historian Brian Walker has argued, this has particularly been the case in Derry. The loss of unionist control of Derry City Council and a decrease of the number of Protestants living in Derry has led to 'a consequent felt need to show Protestant and Unionist solidarity'.[3]

Conclusion

Almost since the siege of Derry took place in 1689, the commemoration of this historic event has been an important way for the Protestant community in Derry to express their cultural identity. The formation of the Apprentice Boys of Derry in the 19th century helped to formalise the commemoration of the siege as a Protestant cultural tradition.

However, the activities of the Apprentice Boys sometimes brought the organisation into conflict with the Catholic community in Derry. Before the outbreak of the Troubles in 1969, the Apprentice Boys parades were

A modern Apprentice Boys parade through Derry to commemorate the shutting of the gates, December 2011

resented by the Catholic community as a symbol of Protestant control of Derry. In two key events relating to the outbreak of the Troubles, the Apprentice Boys played a significant role in antagonising (provoking) the tensions that were already developing as a result of the growth of the civil rights movement. During the Troubles, tensions between the Catholic and Protestant communities ran so high that the activities of the Apprentice Boys were severely restricted.

Since the advent of the peace process in the 1990s, the Apprentice Boys parades have resumed in Derry. The parades are regulated by the independent **Parades Commission** which sets rules about how these events are conducted. The organisation continues to exist as an important symbol of Protestant identity in Ulster.

REVIEW QUESTIONS

1	Approximately how many Apprentice Boys took part in the August parades in the 1950s?
2	Give an example of how the Apprentice Boys parades were a symbol of Protestant authority in Derry.
3	Why did members of the Apprentice Boys consider their organisation to be a symbol of resistance?
4	Explain the term 'gerrymandering' as it applied to Derry in the 1950s and 1960s.
5	What particular custom of the Apprentice Boys did the Catholic community find intimidating?
6	What happened five days before a planned civil rights movement march on 5 October 1968?
7	What did the minister of home affairs do and how did the Apprentice Boys respond to his decision?
8	Why was the Apprentice Boys parade on 12 August 1969 significant?
9	What evidence is there to show that the nationalist community anticipated the parade would turn violent?
10	Why did the Apprentice Boys refuse to cancel their parade?
11	Describe what happened at Waterloo Place on the afternoon of 12 August 1969.
12	What happened with Apprentice Boys parades from 1969?
13	How did Derry City Council try to change the focus of the commemoration of the siege of Derry in 1989?
14	Why did membership of the Apprentice Boys of Derry increase during the era of the Troubles?

EXAMINE THE SOURCES

Source 1

Description of an Apprentice Boys parade in 1964

About 35,000 people visited Derry yesterday, for the 275th anniversary of the Relief of the City in 1689 when the boom across the Foyle was broken and the siege raised in its 106th day.

Just over 5,000 members of the Apprentice Boys took part in a procession through the city. The procession included 100 bands and there were contingents from all parts of Northern Ireland, as well as Co. Donegal, Co. Monaghan, and representatives from Toronto, Philadelphia, Liverpool and Scotland.

The procession, which was 2.5 miles long, took seventy minutes to pass through Carlisle Square.

Five hundred members were initiated [admitted] into the order, including Mr. J.W. Kennedy, M.P., for Cromac, Belfast. More than a dozen men were marching on their 50th "Relief" parade. A feature this year was the colourful decoration of the city by the Apprentice Boys supported by local business houses. The Corporation decorated Craigavon Bridge and Guildhall Square, and lent civic decorations to the Apprentice Boys for the decoration of other streets. Crimson flags were everywhere, including St Columb's Cathedral, which is associated with the siege and the 90 ft. pillar on the walls, erected to the memory of Governor Walker of siege fame.

Source: 'Anniversary of Relief of Derry', *The Irish Times*, 13 August 1964

(a) How many Apprentice Boys took part in the procession?
(b) Where did the Apprentice Boys come from to take part in the procession?
(c) How was the city decorated?
(d) Based on this newspaper article, do you think the Apprentice Boys of Derry was a significant organisation in the 1960s? Give at least three pieces of evidence to support your answer.

Source 2

Impact of the Apprentice Boys on the Catholic community in Derry, 1960s

We resented their [the Apprentice Boys] parading in Derry every 12 August, with their bands and banners and their purple collarettes, jigging through the city centre to celebrate the Siege of Derry and bellow renewed fealty [loyalty] to the glorious, pious and immortal memory of William III. They used to march along the city walls which beetle over Bogside, the ones who had come from outside, from Belfast and Antrim, even Glasgow and Liverpool, leaning over the ramparts to look down at us. Some of them threw pennies. We told one another to 'just ignore them'.

We had our own processions, though on nothing like the same scale, to commemorate the Easter Rising and, sometimes, on St Patrick's Day. Ours did not go through the centre of the city. There was a rigid, unwritten law that Catholics could not march within the city walls. The walls had a mystical significance for Protestants ...

We knew that those who marched on 12 August looked on us with a mixture of hostility and fear. Sometimes the younger ones would sing down from the walls:

> Slaughter, slaughter, holy water,
> Slaughter the papists* one by one.
> We will tear them asunder
> And make them lie under
> The Protestant boys who follow the drum

before joining their contingents as the parade formed up.

Their sense of superiority was based on more than illusion. They were privileged. The lessons about the oppression of Catholics were not academic.

Source: Eamonn McCann, *War and an Irish Town* (Haymarket Books, 2018), pp. 47–48

* Papist is a derogatory term for Catholics.

(a) How did the Catholics of the Bogside react when the Apprentice Boys threw pennies from the city walls?

(b) How were the parades held by the Catholic community different to the Apprentice Boys' parades?

(c) Based on your own knowledge of Derry in the 1960s, what, do you think, does the writer mean by the Apprentice Boys 'looked on us with a mixture of hostility and fear'?

(d) Based on the evidence in this account, describe the writer's attitude to the Apprentice Boys of Derry.

(e) Can this source be described as objective? Explain your answer.

Governor of the Apprentice Boys explains his refusal to cancel parade, August 1969

Dr. Russell Abernethy, the Governor of the Apprentice Boys of Derry, when asked by our reporter yesterday afternoon if they were going ahead with the parade replied that they were.

When his attention was drawn to a report in yesterday's Belfast "Newsletter" that over ninety per cent of the people of Northern Ireland would be glad to see an end to all parades and demonstrations for many months, Dr. Abernethy said that he had not seen the newspaper but he would not be influenced by that report ...

Dr. Abernethy was then asked to comment on the statement by Major Ronald Bunting [a loyalist leader] published yesterday that as a member of the Orange Order and of the Royal Black Institution he (Major Bunting) would be perfectly happy if the leaders of these bodies decided to hold no parades for a period to allow communal disorder to subside.

Dr. Abernethy said: "We do not take our canon law from him. The Apprentice Boys are purely a local historic body. We have no animosity and it is not a question of trailing the coat [provoking conflict], but it would be acknowledging insurrection if any change were to be made concerning the 12th August parade in Derry. It would be bowing to what has been happening of late. Nobody need be apprehensive in so far as those participating in the parade are concerned. We shall do our best to control matters."

Source: Derry Journal, 8 August 1969

(a) According to the *Belfast Newsletter*, what is the view of over 90% of people in Northern Ireland?

(b) How does Abernethy respond to Major Ronald Bunting's comments about parades? Do you find his reaction surprising? Explain your answer.

(c) Explain in your own words why Abernethy refuses to make any changes to arrangements for the 12th August parade.

(d) Based on your knowledge of the Apprentice Boys in 1969, do you agree with Abernethy's view that the organisation was "purely a local historic body"?

View of the General Secretary of the Apprentice Boys of Derry in 1989

Londonderry, as democracy dictates, is now under the control of the Roman Catholic Nationalist and Republican majority in the city. Over recent years they have not shown any more magnanimity [generosity] towards their Protestant Unionist fellow citizens than what they complained of went before when the Unionists were in control. The name of the council was quickly changed from Londonderry (the official name of the city) to Derry, the English version of the old Gaelic name. Nothing was done to prevent the forced exodus [departure] of Protestants by means of murder, intimidation and fear from the west bank city side. In the space of 10 years the Protestant population dwindled from over 20,000 to under 2,000. The predominantly Protestant east bank Waterside part of the city has been largely neglected and starved of resources ...

When the occasions arise, on the two anniversaries each year, thousands come to the city in support of their heritage and culture and to commemorate the fact that their ancestors from all over Ulster found refuge in Londonderry. Aware of what has happened over the past 20 years in Londonderry and also in the Irish Republic, where the Protestant population has dwindled from 10% to under 2%, this is seen as a threat to their British way of life and ethos.

[...] The defenders of Derry fought for civil and religious liberty. Their descendants are fighting the same fight 300 years later.

Source: Derek Miller, *Still Under Siege* (Lurgan: Ulster Society, 1989)

(a) When was this document written?

(b) Give two consequences, according to the author, of the 'Roman Catholic, Nationalist and Republican majority' taking control of the city.

(c) Why do thousands of people come to Londonderry (Derry) on the two anniversaries each year?

(d) How does the author make a connection between what happened in Derry 300 years ago and what is happening in Derry today?

DOCUMENTS-BASED QUESTIONS

The following are three documents-based questions. Use them to practise for your exam.

Question 1 (Higher Level)

Study the two sources below and answer the questions that follow.

Document A

Extract from the autobiography of Paddy Doherty, a leader of the Derry Citizens Defence Association, an organisation set up in July 1969 to represent the residents of the Bogside.

> We [Doherty and Sean Keenan] passed a slogan, 'Give Peace a Chance', daubed in large white letters on the tarmac, as we made our way up Fahan Street towards the Apprentice Boys Hall in the walled city … Our purpose was to make the controlling body of the Apprentice Boys aware of the possibility of serious trouble if the parade were allowed to take place. Their granite Scottish baronial building … dominated its surroundings. It had been constructed on the site of the old monastic settlement which dated from the sixth century and was the world headquarters of the Apprentice Boys of Derry. The meeting was chaired by Doctor Abernathy [sic], who remained silent during the proceedings, leaving the talking to Jim Guy, the secretary, and the Reverend Dickinson, the chaplain. Politely, they explained the precautions they had taken to ensure the march would pass off peacefully. We Bogsiders insisted that the only way to ensure that there would be peace would be to call off the parade. They flatly refused.
>
> Returning to the Bogside, we saw two boys with pots of black paint busily obliterating the white plea for peace from the tarred roadway. No one slept that night. Residents scoured the area for materials for barricades. The Bogside was now on a war footing.
>
> *Source:* Paddy Doherty, *Paddy Bogside* (Cork: Mercier Press, 2001), p. 127

Document B

Prime Minister James Chichester-Clark, speaking in Stormont, explains why his government decided to allow the Apprentice Boys march to proceed.

This is the background against which we had to consider the Apprentice Boys' parade in Londonderry on 12th August. We had suggestions from various quarters that we should restrict it in some way. What were the facts that we had to consider? The demonstration had been held annually for many, many years and had been generally accepted on that basis even by those of opposing views. There was no evidence whatever that those in the parade intended to act in any way irresponsibly. Nor was there any evidence of any organised plan to interfere with them.

Indeed, the indications were that every responsible organisation in the city was directing its efforts to keeping the peace. The hon. Member for Foyle (Mr. [John] Hume) very consistently defended the right of peaceful demonstration within the law. We also had to take into account that if a disciplined and orderly parade was banned a right to parade on that day exercised over countless years might be asserted by other and less well disciplined elements. These grave decisions seem so easy to outsiders but in practice they are always a weighing up of various factors. On balance we decided it was right to give those who had talked so much of peace a chance to live up to it.

Source: Extract from a speech delivered by James Chichester-Clark in Stormont on 14 August 1969

1 Comprehension

(a) According to document A, what was the purpose of Paddy Doherty's visit to the Apprentice Boys Hall?
(b) According to document A, what did the representatives of the Apprentice Boys refuse to do?
(c) In document B, what was 'generally accepted … even by those of opposing views'?
(d) According to document B, what might have happened if 'a disciplined and orderly parade was banned'?

2 Comparison

(a) Do both documents agree that efforts were being made to keep the peace in Derry during the Apprentice Boys parade? Give reasons for your answer, referring to both documents.
(b) Do both documents agree that violence was likely to break out at the Apprentice Boys parade? Give reasons for your answer, referring to both documents.

3 Criticism

(a) Does document A show the value of biographical material as a historical source?
(b) Do both documents show that the Apprentice Boys of Derry was regarded as an important organisation in Northern Ireland?

4 Contextualisation

To what extent were the activities of the Apprentice Boys of Derry divisive?

Question 2 (Higher Level)

Study the two sources below and answer the questions that follow.

Document A

An *Irish Press* journalist describes what happened at the Apprentice Boys parade in Derry, 12 August 1969.

The clashes had started in early afternoon at Waterloo Place, which the Apprentice Boys' parade had to pass on its traditional route. Protestant spectators of the parade were infuriated when Catholic youths from Bogside jeered the parade and sang rival songs – most of which were drowned out by the booming drums of the brass bands.

"Shoot them", "Whip them", screamed an hysterical woman at the Bogside group, massed behind the police barriers. Then the stones started to fly from the youths gathered at the junction of William Street and Waterloo Place. It was the spark they all feared would turn the day into disaster.

A hail of stones rained on the police, who had taken out their shields. Many stones fell among the marching Apprentice Boys, making them run for cover. But they reasserted themselves quickly and continued to run the gauntlet grim-faced. The bands played louder, the flutes screached [sic] more defiantly and the drums rolled more menacingly.

Civil Rights stewards persuaded most of the youths to move back down William Street. At the junction with Rossville Street a barricade was quickly assembled, while the most vicious stone throwing so far broke out between Catholic demonstrators and police at the corner of near by Sackville Street.

Source: The Irish Press, 13 August 1969

Document B

A *Times* journalist also describes what happened at the Apprentice Boys parade in Derry, 12 August 1969.

This time I and a number of other English reporters saw exactly how it started and we have no doubts. All day yesterday the noise of "The Sash" and "Derry's Walls" played by flute bands, pipe bands and accordion bands had irritated the Bogside Catholics as it floated down from the walls above them ...

Although the marchers were highly disciplined and impeccably behaved many of the Bogside Catholics said they felt like animals in a zoo as bowler-hatted apprentice boys and their wives in Sunday best gazed down upon them from the walls. No one, it appeared, had suggested to the police or to the organizers that this little touch of provocation could have been avoided or that the bands might come down to a drum beat while they passed within earshot of the Bogside.

In Waterloo Square, where the now notorious William Street runs from Bogside on to the route of the march, the inevitable happened.

A group of Catholics appeared first to stone, then to jeer, then to catapult their marbles, then to throw bricks.

The next steps were familiar and predictable: first the modest police barricade, then the return fire from some Protestants, then a deliberate attack by a party of masked Catholics on another section of the parade, then the police in riot kit pushing the Catholics back and the familiar message being passed back through the area that the Bogside "was under attack".

Source: The Times, 14 August 1969

1 Comprehension

(a) According to document A, why did the Protestant spectators of the parade become 'infuriated'?

(b) In document A, what happened at the junction with Rossville Street?

(c) In document B, what songs were played by the Apprentice Boys' bands?

(d) According to document B, how did the 'Bogside Catholics' feel as the march passed along the city walls?

2 Comparison

(a) Do both documents agree that some aspects of the Apprentice Boys parade were intimidating? Give reasons for your answer, referring to both documents.

(b) Do both documents agree on how the rioting broke out during the parade? Give reasons for your answer, referring to both documents.

3 Criticism

(a) Which document gives the clearer idea of what happened at the Apprentice Boys parade?

(b) Do you agree that both documents show that newspaper accounts are objective and reliable sources for the historian?

4 Contextualisation

Discuss how the Apprentice Boys of Derry helped to express Protestant culture and identity in Northern Ireland in the period 1949–1993.

Study the two sources below and answer the questions that follow.

Document A

Fergus Pyle's depiction, for *The Irish Times* (Dublin), of the Derry Apprentice Boys march, 12 August 1967.

On Saturday it rained with a particular intensity in Derry, but the Apprentice Boys marched their appointed route with their banners fluttering and their bands pumping out the traditional tunes. It is, in its way, a great folk festival. And it has a good humour which is not so marked in other celebrations in Ulster.

They wore a traditional uniform of bowler hats and crimson sashes – really collarettes – and large cuffs, to show what position the wearer holds in the club. On either side of the flags, men march with swords drawn.

In the morning, a large crowd attended a service at the cathedral to hear a sermon counselling restraint towards people of different religious persuasions, with steadfastness in defence of the Protestant heritage.

From then on, the streets were filled with marching men, and the air was filled with music from silver, accordion, pipe and flute bands. The tunes were the traditional ones – "Derry's Walls", naturally enough, "The Boyne Water", and – incongruously – the Jacobite hit, "Will Ye No' Come Back Again".

Source: The Irish Times, 14 August 1967

Document B

Max Hastings, who reported from Northern Ireland for *The Evening Standard* (London), wrote about the 1969 march.

> The solemn procession of the Derry Apprentice Boys began, in perfect tranquility, on the morning of August 12th. There were thousands of them, in their sober suits and bowler hats and flute bands and drum bands, their wives watching from the city walls, all dressed up in Sunday best.
>
> The Catholics, in the Bogside below the city, complained that they felt like animals in a zoo, as spectators and Apprentice Boys gazed down over the parapets, to peer into the Catholic cauldron below. In the Bogside they could hear the sound of bands, and the Protestant tunes – the endless renderings of "The Wearing of the Sash" and "Derry's Walls".
>
> By general consent, and after much hard work by the moderate Catholic leaders, most Catholics stayed at home during the march, sick of Protestants and police cordons and riot tenders and drumbeating. But they were irritated, ill-humoured and apprehensive.
>
> *Source:* Max Hastings, *Ulster 1969: The Fight for Civil Rights in Northern Ireland* (London: Gollancz, 1970)

1 Comprehension

(a) According to document A, what was the traditional uniform of the marchers?
(b) From document B, what forms of music accompanied the marchers?
(c) According to document B, why did the Bogsiders complain that they felt like animals in a zoo?
(d) According to document A, what tune was out of place?

2 Comparison

(a) Document B describes the Apprentice Boys march as 'a solemn procession'. Does document A support or contradict that description? Give reasons for your answer.
(b) From the evidence of the documents, would you agree that religion was important both to Apprentice Boys and to Bogsiders? Give reasons for your answer.

3 Criticism

(a) How does document B show the tensions that had arisen in Northern Ireland between the dates of the two marches, 1967 and 1969? Refer to both documents in your answer.
(b) How do the given documents illustrate strengths and weaknesses of the work of journalists as historical source material?

4 Contextualisation

What was the significance of the activities of the Apprentice Boys of Derry for both Unionists and Nationalists in Northern Ireland?

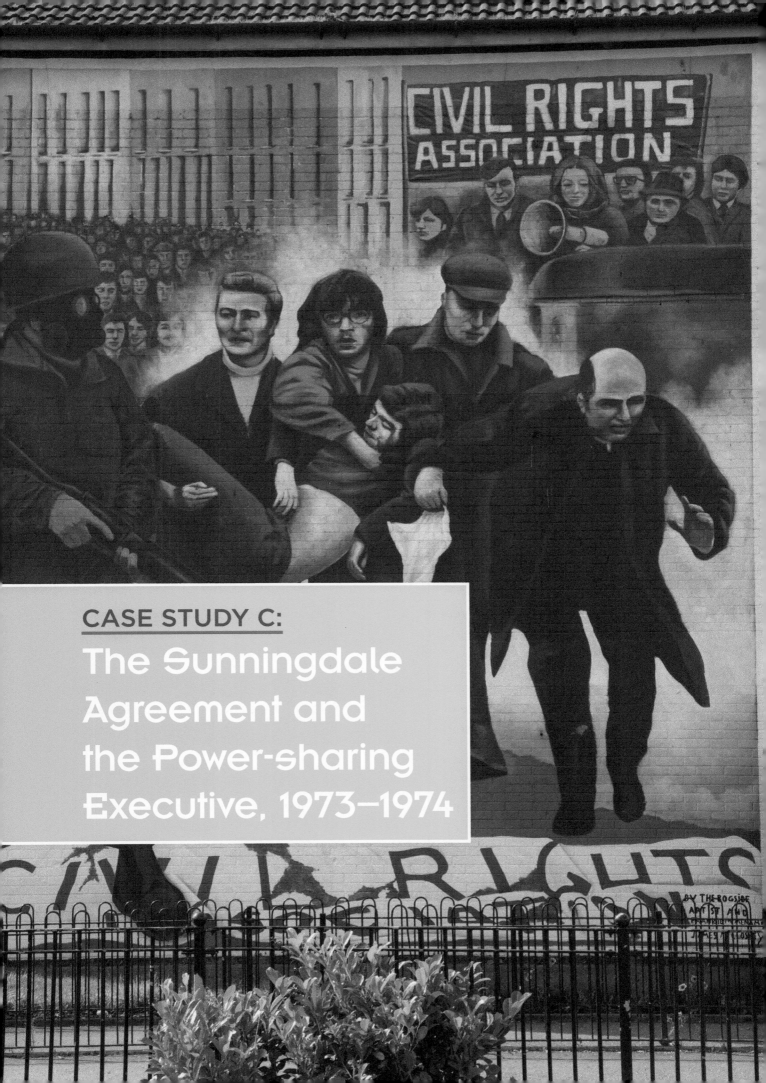

CASE STUDY C:

The Sunningdale Agreement and the Power-sharing Executive, 1973–1974

7 Background to the Sunningdale Agreement 1971–1972

Violence intensified in Northern Ireland and in 1972 the British government decided on direct rule from Westminster as a temporary measure while a political settlement was negotiated. Negotiations resulted in the Sunningdale Agreement in 1973. This chapter looks at the events leading up to the Sunningdale Agreement.

Violence in Derry intensified

Useful terms

➤ Internment Imprisonment without trial.

➤ Marching season A period every year in Northern Ireland when members of organisations such as the Orange Order and the Apprentice Boys of Derry take part in parades across Northern Ireland.

➤ Paramilitary organisation An organisation for which civilians organise themselves in the style of an army. Such organisations are often illegal and in Northern Ireland they included dissident groups such as the Provisional Irish Republican Army (IRA) and the Ulster Defence Association (UDA).

By the end of 1972, the situation in Northern Ireland had reached crisis point. Violence had intensified since the outbreak of the Troubles in 1969 and in 1972 alone almost 500 people died as a result of the conflict. The introduction of internment in August 1971 and the events of Bloody Sunday in January 1972 persuaded the British government that Northern Ireland could no longer govern itself. Direct rule from Westminster was introduced as a temporary measure. A political solution was then sought in an effort to bring an end to the conflict.

> **? KEY QUESTION**
> What were the key developments that led to the negotiation of the Sunningdale Agreement?

What led to the introduction of direct rule?

Introduction of internment, August 1971

In March 1971, **James Chichester-Clark** resigned as prime minister of Northern Ireland in protest at the failure of the British government to provide the security measures he had requested. He was replaced by **Brian Faulkner**, who wanted to introduce the controversial security policy of internment. Large-scale rioting occurred across Northern Ireland during the marching season in the summer of 1971. In response, **internment** was introduced by Faulkner on 9 August 1971.

Rioting in Derry in July 1971

Faulkner's aim with internment was to end violence, but his policy had the opposite effect. It quickly became clear that internment was one-sided. **British soldiers** and **RUC officers** who participated in **Operation Demetrius** on 9 August arrested only those they suspected of being members of the IRA. Opposition to internment led to the worst day of violence in Northern Ireland since the battle of the Bogside (see p. 58) on 10 August, when an estimated 2,000 families in Belfast were forced to flee their homes. From the introduction of internment until the end of 1971, 150 people died as a result of the conflict.

Bloody Sunday, January 1972

The growing conflict reached a new low on 30 January 1972 at a protest march against internment held in Derry. The march turned violent and **British paratroopers** shot dead 13 unarmed civilians. Another victim later died in hospital from his injuries. The events of **Bloody Sunday** prompted international outrage. There were violent protests across Northern Ireland and in Dublin, where protestors burned down the British Embassy.

Brian Faulkner, prime minister of Northern Ireland, introduced internment following widespread rioting in July and August 1971

Bernadette Devlin, MP for mid-Ulster, addressing an anti-internment rally in September 1971. Internment caused outrage among the nationalists as many of those arrested had no connection to the IRA

British soldiers marching away civilians in the aftermath of Bloody Sunday.

British paratrooper attacks an anti-internment protestor on Bloody Sunday, 30 January 1972

Direct rule is introduced

One outcome of the events of Bloody Sunday was that the British prime minister **Edward Heath** became convinced that Faulkner's government could no longer control the security situation. He introduced direct rule on 28 March, whereby the parliament at Stormont ceased to function and Northern Ireland was ruled directly from Westminster. Faulkner resigned and Heath appointed **William Whitelaw** to the new position of **secretary of state for Northern Ireland**.

What was Northern Ireland like under direct rule?

William Whitelaw and the Provisional IRA

At first, Whitelaw thought that the best solution to ending the violence was to introduce measures that would improve relations with the nationalist community. Hundreds of internees were released from prison and those who remained were given special category status. Following discussions with **John Hume**, the Provisional IRA agreed to a ceasefire on 26 June. Provisional IRA negotiators were flown to London where they entered into discussions with William Whitelaw. Whitelaw could not meet the IRA demand for British withdrawal from Northern Ireland and the talks collapsed within two days.

William Whitelaw, first secretary of state for Northern Ireland

Bloody Friday, 21 July 1972

The IRA ceasefire ended and the campaign of violence resumed with renewed intensity. On 21 July 1972, in one of the worst days of violence during the Troubles, the IRA detonated 20 bombs within 65 minutes in Belfast, killing nine people and seriously injuring 130 people. This day became known as **Bloody Friday**.

Operation Motorman

There was widespread condemnation of the explosions on Bloody Friday. Whitelaw responded by implementing a British Army plan called **Operation Motorman**. On 29 and 30 July, thousands of British soldiers were flown into Northern Ireland. Their aim was to take back control of the 'no go areas', which were located mostly in nationalist areas of Belfast and Derry. They were so called because it was impossible for the British Army to enter these districts without rioting breaking out. Whitelaw had anticipated that nationalists living in the 'no go areas' would strongly resist the arrival of the military, however the British Army were able to take control of these areas with ease.

The scene at Cavehill Road Shopping Centre in Belfast following a Provisional IRA bombing on 21 July 1972. Nine people died and 130 were injured as a result of explosions on that day

Some nationalist areas of Derry and Belfast were 'no go areas' before Operation Motorman was implemented

Unionist opposition to direct rule

Unionists were deeply unhappy with the introduction of direct rule. The Stormont parliament was the centre of unionist power in Northern Ireland and they considered the decision to shut it down as a betrayal by the British government.

The **Ulster Vanguard movement** was an organisation led by **William Craig** within the Unionist Party. Vanguard was in favour of a semi-independent Northern Ireland and was opposed to giving concessions to the Catholic community. In protest against the introduction of direct rule, the Vanguard organised a two-day **workers' strike** in late March 1972 which brought Northern Ireland to a standstill. An estimated 100,000 people took part in a rally at Stormont during the strike.

William Craig, leader of the Ulster Vanguard movement, at a rally at Belfast City Hall

Growth in loyalist paramilitary organisations

In 1971 a loyalist paramilitary organisation, the **Ulster Defence Association (UDA)**, was founded in Belfast. The stated aim of the UDA was to defend Protestant communities from attack by republicans.

Membership of the UDA increased rapidly throughout 1972. Many members of the Protestant community joined following the introduction of internment, as the increase in violence persuaded them that the police and army could no longer protect them. Membership also increased with the introduction of direct rule. Those who joined were opposed to the shutting

Ulster Defence Association march on the Shankill Road, Belfast in 1972

down of the Stormont parliament and saw the release of internees by William Whitelaw as evidence that the government was siding with the Catholic community.

Towards the end of 1972 there was an increase in the number of sectarian killings of Catholics by the UDA, and by the end of the year 120 people had been killed by loyalists.

Why was a political solution needed?

With the failure of talks with the IRA, William Whitelaw decided that finding a political solution to the conflict was the best strategy for ending violence. A political solution was required because:

▸ The introduction of direct rule was intended only as a **temporary measure**. Whitelaw wanted to reintroduce self-government to Northern Ireland but this time with reforms that would more fairly represent the interests of the nationalist community.

▸ The conflict had reached crisis point. In July 1972 alone, 95 people died as a result of the violence. Membership of republican and loyalist paramilitary organisations was increasing rapidly. Whitelaw hoped that a political settlement would provide a solution that would help to end the violent conflict.

▸ The success of Operation Motorman and the ease with which the British Army took control of the 'no go areas' weakened the position of the IRA and convinced Whitelaw that the time was ripe for securing a political solution.

This was the background against which political negotiations began that eventually led to the signing of the **Sunningdale Agreement**.

REVIEW QUESTIONS

1	What was internment and why was it introduced to Northern Ireland in 1971?
2	Why was internment considered one-sided?
3	Describe what happened in Derry on 30 January 1972.
4	What was one of the main outcomes of Bloody Sunday?
5	What actions of William Whitelaw persuaded the Provisional IRA to declare a ceasefire?
6	Why did talks between the Provisional IRA and the British government collapse?
7	What was the aim of Operation Motorman?
8	What was the Ulster Vanguard movement?
9	Give two reasons why membership of the UDA increased rapidly throughout 1972.
10	Explain why William Whitelaw reached the conclusion that a political settlement was needed for Northern Ireland.

EXAMINE THE SOURCE

Protestant workers strike in response to direct rule, 28 March 1972

Many thousands of Protestant workers rallied behind the Ulster Vanguard movement yesterday and showed their contempt [disdain] for the Westminster Government's direct rule proposals by holding strikes and protest meetings in many centres throughout the North.

The biggest demonstration was in front of City Hall, Belfast, where the Vanguard leader, Mr. William Craig, M.P., told over 15,000 people that the movement would mount a campaign to bring back a parliament, with even greater powers, to Northern Ireland. "We will have to fight and we will fight," he declared.

The general strike, which is planned to continued today, brought industry, commerce and public services to an almost complete halt. All over the North electricity supplies were cut to one-third of the normal output when workers failed to start work, and what was left had to be distributed on a rota basis in different areas.

The strike was accompanied by outbreaks of violence by Loyalists, particularly in Portadown, which was sealed off by barricades last night.

Because of the power cuts, and in some cases a water shortage, many factories which might have continued production, had to close down.

[...]

There were widespread reports of carloads of men driving around Belfast warning people to close their premises and it is known that in several cases people who turned up for work were told they could go home because of bomb scares at their work places. All the scares were hoaxes.

Source: The Irish Times, 28 March 1972

(a) How did Protestant workers and the Ulster Vanguard movement respond to the British government's proposed introduction of direct rule?
(b) Who addressed the rally at City Hall and how many people were in attendance?
(c) What caused electricity supplies to reduce to one-third of the normal output?
(d) What actions were taken to ensure that workplaces in Belfast shut down?
(e) In your opinion, what challenges did the British government face in finding a political solution to the conflict in Northern Ireland? Support your answer with evidence from the document.

8 Negotiating the Sunningdale Agreement, 1973

This chapter examines the main political parties in Northern Ireland in 1972, with a particular focus on the parties that took part in the negotiation of the Sunningdale Agreement. An assembly, power-sharing executive and Council of Ireland were key elements of the agreement that was signed in December 1973.

Signing of the Sunningdale Agreement

Useful terms

▸ **Consensus** Where different individuals or groups have opposing views but manage to reach an agreement that is acceptable to all parties.

▸ **Green paper** A discussion paper published by a government. It usually contains an outline of a particular issue and puts forward for debate ideas on how to resolve this issue.

▸ **Power-sharing** A system of government where political parties with opposing views agree to form a government together, known as an **executive**. This system allowed for the special circumstances of Northern Ireland. Power-sharing meant that unionist and nationalist representatives would govern Northern Ireland together. This allowed nationalists – traditionally a minority group in Northern Ireland – to have a strong voice in government.

▸ **Self-determination** The right of a people to determine their own national identity.

▸ **White paper** A policy document published by a government. It contains a formal statement of government policy on a particular issue.

Main political parties in Northern Ireland in 1972

Nationalist

Provisional Sinn Féin The party could trace its origins back to 1905, when it was established by Arthur Griffith. The party split into Official Sinn Féin and Provisional Sinn Féin in January 1970. The split occurred because of concerns by some that the Dublin-based leadership of the party was not taking enough action to assist nationalists in Northern Ireland. Provisional Sinn Féin sought the withdrawal of the British government and security forces from Northern Ireland and the creation of a 32-county Irish republic. The party was not invited to talks associated with the Sunningdale Agreement because of its close associations with the IRA.

Gerry Fitt was leader of the SDLP at the time of its foundation in 1970 and was party leader until 1979

Social Democratic and Labour Party (SDLP) was founded in August 1970 and was the main nationalist party in Northern Ireland in the 1970s. Many of the founding members had been involved in the civil rights movement in the 1960s. The SDLP wanted to achieve Irish unity by peaceful means. The party leader was Gerry Fitt and John Hume was chief strategist.

Centre

Alliance Party of Northern Ireland was founded in April 1970 as an alternative to the traditional nationalist and unionist parties in Northern Ireland. The Alliance Party was unique in that it attracted support from both the Catholic and Protestant communities. The Alliance Party aimed to end the sectarian divide in the region and believed that Northern Ireland should remain part of the UK.

Oliver Napier was the first leader of the Alliance Party

Northern Ireland Labour Party (NILP) was founded in 1924 and had links to the Labour Party in Britain. The party was seen as a party of the centre because its membership came from both the unionist and nationalist communities.

Unionist

Ulster Unionist Party (UUP) was founded in 1905 and it was the main party of government from the foundation of the Northern Ireland parliament in 1921 up until the introduction of direct rule in 1972. All six prime ministers of Northern Ireland during this period were also leaders of the

Unionist Party. The core belief of the party was maintaining the union between Great Britain and Northern Ireland. The leader of the party from March 1971 to January 1974 was Brian Faulkner.

Democratic Unionist Party (DUP) was founded at the Ulster Hall in Belfast by Ian Paisley in October 1971. Its views were more radical than those of the UUP. Many of its members were associated with Paisley's Free Presbyterian Church of Ulster and the party was strongly opposed to allowing nationalists to have any influence over the governing of Northern Ireland.

Ian Paisley founded the DUP in 1970

There were many steps in the negotiation of a political settlement for Northern Ireland that eventually resulted in the Sunningdale Agreement. Negotiations in late 1972 and early 1973 produced a number of key proposals from the British government. Northern Ireland would have a new assembly (parliament) and be governed by an executive where power would be shared between unionists and nationalists. A Council of Ireland would be established to develop north–south relations. Talks in December 1973 resulted in the Sunningdale Agreement which formalised a political settlement for Northern Ireland.

> **? KEY QUESTION**
> What were the main events that led to the creation of a power-sharing executive in Northern Ireland?

How was a power-sharing executive created?

Darlington conference, September 1972

In September 1972 Whitelaw held talks at **Darlington** in England to discuss a political settlement for Northern Ireland. The talks were attended by the **Ulster Unionist Party**, the **Northern Ireland Labour Party** and the **Alliance Party of Northern Ireland**. The **Socialist, Democratic and Labour Party** were invited to attend but refused to do so because they were opposed to the ongoing

Security was tight at the inter-party conference held by William Whitelaw at the Europa Lodge Hotel, in Darlington, England

policy of internment. They were also disappointed that members of the Irish government had not been invited to the discussions.

Green paper, The Future of Northern Ireland

The main outcome of the Darlington conference was the publication of a discussion document or green paper, ***The Future of Northern Ireland***, by the British government. The document outlined the current political situation in Northern Ireland and put forward proposals on how political issues could be resolved. The key points of the document were:

> **Status of Northern Ireland:** It was recognised that Northern Ireland might eventually change its constitutional status to become part of a united Ireland. However, it was acknowledged that this would happen only with the consent of the majority of people in Northern Ireland.

> **Power-sharing:** The document stated that 'minority interests' should have a role in the government and administration of Northern Ireland. This idea later became known as power-sharing. It meant that members of both the majority unionist and minority nationalist communities would participate in government together.

Front cover of the green paper published by the British government in 1972

> **'The Irish dimension':** Up until this point the British government had mostly rejected the attempts of the Irish government to become involved in matters relating to Northern Ireland. This document was significant because it acknowledged that the south was entitled to have an interest in any political agreement relating to Northern Ireland. The new willingness to consult with the Irish government in relation to Northern Ireland became known as 'the Irish dimension'.

The significance of *The Future of Northern Ireland* was that it 'marked a turning point in the policy of the British Government on the Northern Ireland problem'.[1] Many of the ideas in the document formed the basis of British government policy on Northern Ireland for decades to come and helped to shape future agreements.

The nationalist SDLP were particularly impressed by 'the Irish dimension' aspect of the document and from this point were willing to become involved in discussions on a political settlement. Within the UUP, the document was opposed by the Vanguard movement. They were against power-sharing and 'the Irish dimension' as they felt too many concessions were being given to Catholics.

Border poll, March 1973

The British government decided to hold a **border poll** in Northern Ireland on 8 March 1973. This was a vote on whether or not Northern Ireland should remain part of the United Kingdom. As there was a majority unionist population in Northern Ireland, a result in favour of remaining in the UK was essentially guaranteed. The purpose of holding the poll was to reassure unionists that their position was secure before a new political settlement was put in place.

Nationalist parties encouraged Catholics to boycott the border poll. Only 59% of the electorate voted in the poll and the result was 99% in favour of staying in the UK.

On the day of the border poll, the Provisional IRA detonated two car bombs in central London, including one outside the Old Bailey courthouse

White paper, Northern Ireland: Constitutional Proposals

With the border poll showing a clear majority in favour of remaining in the UK, Whitelaw moved to publish a white paper, ***Northern Ireland: Constitutional Proposals***. The white paper stated British government policy on setting up new political structures in Northern Ireland. Three key institutions were to be established:

1 Assembly: The assembly was the name given to a new parliament for Northern Ireland. Members of the new parliament were to be elected by proportional representation.
2 Executive: The executive would form the government of Northern Ireland. The power to legislate on certain matters would be transferred from Westminster to the executive. The executive would involve **cross-community power-sharing**, meaning that it would have representatives from both the Protestant and Catholic communities. The executive could be formed only if the secretary of state was satisfied that it would have widespread support across Northern Ireland.
3 Council of Ireland: A Council of Ireland would be established to promote **north–south cooperation**. Negotiations on the structure and workings of the Council of Ireland were to take place after elections to the assembly.

Responses to the white paper were mixed. On the unionist side, the leader of the Unionist Party, Brian Faulkner, described it as a 'constructive document' and thought that some points could be negotiated further. The white paper was outright rejected by William Craig's Vanguard movement. Aspects such as sharing power with Catholics and allowing the Irish government to have a say in the affairs of Northern Ireland were seen as unacceptable. In protest, Craig's supporters broke away from the Ulster Unionist Party to form their own party, the **Vanguard Unionist Progressive Party**. For similar reasons the document was deemed unacceptable by Ian Paisley's DUP.

The document was broadly welcomed by the SDLP and the Alliance Party. For the first time in the history of the Northern Ireland state, a power-sharing executive would give representation to both nationalists and unionists in government.

Assembly elections, June 1973

The British government proceeded with elections to the new assembly, held on 28 June 1973. The results showed that unionist support for the proposals was divided. Unionists against power-sharing won 26 seats and members of the UUP who supported Faulkner won 24 seats. The SDLP won 19 seats, establishing them as the main party for nationalists. The results for the centre parties were disappointing, with the Alliance Party winning eight seats and the NILP gaining just one seat. The first meeting of the assembly was held in July.

Formation of the executive, November 1973

The next step was to negotiate the formation of the power-sharing executive that would govern Northern Ireland. The executive was announced in November 1973 after negotiations at Stormont Castle. It would consist of:

» Six Ulster Unionist ministers
» Four SDLP ministers
» One Alliance Party minister.

The leader of the executive, known as the **chief executive**, was Brian Faulkner, the UUP leader. The **deputy chief executive** was Gerry Fitt, leader of the SDLP.

> **? KEY QUESTION**
> What happened at the Sunningdale conference and what were the main points of the Sunningdale Agreement?

What was the Sunningdale Agreement?

Sunningdale conference

The final step in achieving a political agreement was to bring together the executive, the British government and the Irish government to agree on how the proposed **Council of Ireland** would function. Negotiations took place at a civil service training centre in **Sunningdale** in **Berkshire, England** in December 1973.

The newly elected Fine Gael Taoiseach, **Liam Cosgrave**, attended the talks, along with minister of foreign affairs, **Garret FitzGerald** and other ministers.

Unionist party leader Brian Faulkner with Taoiseach Liam Cosgrave during the Sunningdale negotiations, 9 December 1973

Shortly before the talks began, William Whitelaw was replaced as secretary of state for Northern Ireland by **Francis Pym**. The Conservative prime minister **Edward Heath** was also in attendance. Representatives of the UUP, the SDLP and the Alliance Party were involved in negotiations.

One issue of concern for unionists attending the talks was Articles 2 and 3 of the **Irish constitution**. These articles laid claim to Northern Ireland as part of the national territory. Unionists felt that this threatened their right to **self-determination**. They wanted reassurances from the Irish government that it accepted there could be no change to the status of Northern Ireland without the consent of the majority of people in Northern Ireland. They were also concerned

Signing of the Sunningdale Agreement. The Taoiseach Liam Cosgrave shakes hands with the prime minister Ted Heath, as (from left) Oliver Napier (Alliance Party), Brian Faulkner (Unionist) and Gerry Fitt (SDLP) look on

that greater cooperation between the government in the north and south, such as the Council of Ireland, might eventually lead to Irish unity.

The SDLP were strongly in favour of the Council of Ireland. They felt that nationalists would give support to institutions like the assembly and the executive only if a north–south body was part of the final agreement.

The main points of the agreement concluded on 9 December 1973 were:

- ▸▸ **Council of Ireland:** There would be a two-tier Council of Ireland. The first tier, the Council of Ministers, would be made up of Irish government ministers and ministers from the Northern Ireland executive. The second tier, the consultative assembly, would be made up of 30 members of the Irish parliament and 30 members of the Northern Ireland assembly. The powers of the Council were not clearly defined, however. Reference was made to 'harmonisation' between north and south on issues of mutual interest such as membership of the European Economic Community. However, the powers of the Council to make policy relating to issues of mutual interest was not outlined in detail.
- ▸▸ **Status of Northern Ireland:** The Irish government could not meet the unionist demand of removing Articles 2 and 3 from the Irish constitution. This could be done only by **referendum** and the Irish delegates thought that such a proposal would be rejected by Irish voters. However, the Irish government included a statement in the agreement which declared that 'it fully accepts and solemnly declares that there would be no change in the status of Northern Ireland until a majority of people desired a change in that status'.
- ▸▸ **Law and order:** It was agreed that there would be greater cooperation between the police forces of Northern Ireland and the Republic of Ireland on security issues.

Sunningdale Agreement: strengths and weaknesses

The Sunningdale conference brought together different groups that held often strongly opposing views and they succeeded in achieving a **consensus**. For the first time, the Irish government played a significant role in negotiating an agreement relating to Northern Ireland.

The powers of the Council of Ireland were not clearly defined. This gave hope to the nationalist SDLP that the Council could, over time, lead to close cooperation between north and south on issues of mutual interest. However, uncertainty over the powers of the Council also led to growing fears among unionists that the Council of Ireland would be the way in which they would eventually be forced into accepting a united Ireland.

Those involved in negotiating the Sunningdale Agreement underestimated the strength of unionist opposition to the Council of Ireland that would become very evident in the early months of 1974.

REVIEW QUESTIONS

1	Why did members of the SDLP refuse to attend the Darlington conference?
2	Explain the concept of power-sharing in relation to Northern Ireland in the 1970s.
3	What was 'the Irish dimension'?
4	Why was the green paper, The Future of Northern Ireland, considered significant?
5	What was the purpose of the British government holding a border poll in March 1974?
6	What three institutions were to be formed according to the white paper, Northern Ireland: Constitutional Proposals?
7	Why were the white paper proposals rejected by William Craig and the Vanguard movement?
8	Describe the make-up of the Northern Ireland executive, announced in November 1973.
9	Who was present at the Sunningdale conference on behalf of the Irish government?
10	What was one of the main issues for unionists that emerged during the Sunningdale negotiations?
11	Describe the workings of the Council of Ireland as agreed at Sunningdale.
12	How did the Irish government try to resolve unionists' concerns about the status of Northern Ireland?
13	Why was the SDLP in favour of the Council of Ireland and why did unionists have concerns about the Council of Ireland?

EXAMINE THE SOURCES

Source 1

Garret FitzGerald, Irish minister of foreign affairs, on the Sunningdale conference

Sunningdale Park in Berkshire is a civil service college. The conference itself was to take place in the principal block, Northcote House, and the participants ... were accommodated in residences on the estate some five hundred yards away.

Northcote House, a 1930s mansion ... is constructed around a mock 'great hall'. From the balcony that surrounds the hall at first-floor level and off which the offices of the Irish and British delegations were housed, the floor below was like a stage set; from our vantage point we could observe the entrances and exits of other participants, and speculate why, and concerning what, A was talking to B, or C sedulously [carefully] avoiding D.

The conference was a unique occasion. Never before had the political leaders of the British and Irish states and of the two communities in Northern Ireland been gathered together in one place. Some 120 people attended, including a dozen members of the Irish and British cabinets and a score of politicians representing the Ulster Unionist, Alliance and SDLP parties in Northern Ireland.

On Thursday morning we met a number of our colleagues at breakfast. I was with Brian Faulkner when Liam Cosgrave arrived and joined our table. They had already met in the hunting field, I gathered, and within minutes they were chatting away about mutual acquaintances. They were quickly on good terms, strolling around the grounds together during breaks in the meetings.

Source: Garret FitzGerald, *All in a Life* (Dublin: Gill and Macmillan, 1991), p. 211

(a) What were the buildings at Sunningdale Park used for?

(b) What could Garret Fitzgerald and his colleagues see from their vantage point?

(c) How many people were in attendance at the conference?

(d) Why was the conference 'a unique occasion'?

(e) Based on your knowledge of the period, who was Brian Faulkner and who was Liam Cosgrave?

(f) Based on the evidence in this document, what can you say about the relationship between Faulkner and Cosgrave?

(g) Do you think this document is useful in helping historians to understand the workings of the Sunningdale conference? Explain your answer with reference to the document.

Noel Dorr, an Irish civil servant, reflects on the importance of the Sunningdale Agreement

I do think that Sunningdale was important. Although it did not succeed in its immediate objective, I believe that it marked an important turning point in the approach of both the British and Irish governments to the problem of Northern Ireland. Furthermore, ideas and concepts that were developed around the time of Sunningdale – on issues such as power-sharing and north–south relations – remained relevant and some were drawn on as building blocks in the settlement achieved eventually in Northern Ireland some 25 years later.

Source: Noel Dorr, *The Search for Peace in Northern Ireland: Sunningdale* (Dublin: Royal Irish Academy, 2017), p. 4

(a) What ideas developed during the Sunningdale negotiations 'remained relevant'?

(b) How long was it before a settlement was eventually achieved relating to Northern Ireland?

(c) Based on your knowledge of this period, why, do you think, did Noel Dorr describe the Sunningdale Agreement as 'an important turning point in the approach of both the British and Irish governments to the problem of Northern Ireland'?

9 Response to Sunningdale and the collapse of the power-sharing institutions, 1973–1974

A British soldier guards a petrol tank during the Ulster Workers' Council strike, May 1974

Increasing opposition to the Sunningdale Agreement led to a general strike that eventually resulted in the collapse of the executive. This chapter looks at the events that ended power-sharing in Northern Ireland.

Useful terms

▸ **Partition** The border dividing the 26 counties of the south of Ireland from the six counties of the north of Ireland, first introduced in 1921.

▸ **Reconciliation** A healing of divisions between two sides.

At first, the Sunningdale Agreement was seen as a breakthrough in resolving the conflict in Northern Ireland. The assembly and the executive were up and running by January 1974. However, it quickly became apparent that a growing number of unionists were strongly opposed to aspects of the agreement such as power-sharing and the Council of Ireland. This became very clear following general election results in February 1974, with a majority of unionists supporting anti-Sunningdale candidates. The Ulster Workers' Council strike, which lasted for 14 days in May 1974, eventually forced the collapse of the executive.

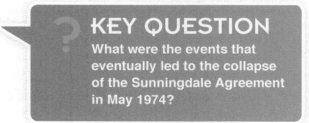

? KEY QUESTION
What were the events that eventually led to the collapse of the Sunningdale Agreement in May 1974?

What was the response to the Sunningdale Agreement?

'Save Ulster' rally

While the conference at Sunningdale was still ongoing, a rally was held at the **Ulster Hall** on 6 December 1973 attended by unionists opposed to power-sharing. At the rally the DUP leader Ian Paisley, the leader of the Vanguard movement William Craig, and some members of the Orange Order decided to come together to found the **United Ulster Unionist Council** to work together to oppose the Sunningdale Agreement.

Nationalist response

The Sunningdale Agreement was broadly welcomed by the nationalist community. The assembly and the executive would give nationalists a say in the governing of Northern Ireland for the first time. The Council of Ireland was seen as a positive development in strengthening links with the south.

Ian Paisley speaking at the 'Save Ulster' rally, 6 December 1973

The agreement was opposed by Sinn Féin and the IRA, however. They objected to the Council of Ireland as they believed that by recognising two governments on the island of Ireland, the Council would reinforce **partition**. In response to Sunningdale the IRA carried out a series of bombings in London, detonating three bombs in the city on 18 December.

What happened when the executive first took office in 1974?

First meeting of the Northern Ireland executive, 1 January 1974

The power-sharing executive took office on 1 January 1974 with Faulkner as chief executive and Fitt as deputy chief executive. There were ministers from the Unionist, SDLP and Alliance parties, including John Hume of the SDLP as minister of commerce. The meeting of the executive was a sign of hope for **reconciliation** but the events that followed would greatly weaken its authority.

Harry West, an anti-Sunningdale Unionist who replaced Brian Faulkner as leader of the party in January 1974

Meeting of the Ulster Unionist Council, 4 January 1974

It soon became clear that the terms of the Sunningdale Agreement were unacceptable to the majority of unionists. Just three days after the first meeting of the executive the Ulster Unionist Council, the governing body of the Ulster Unionist Party, met to vote on a motion condemning the Council of Ireland. The motion was carried and Faulkner was forced to resign as leader of the party. He was replaced by Harry West who was opposed to power-sharing. The authority of the executive was now weakened, as its leader no longer had the majority support of his own party.

First meeting of the Northern Ireland assembly, 22 January 1974

The first meeting of the assembly on 22 January 1974 descended into chaos when Ian Paisley and his supporters disrupted the meeting and had to be forcibly removed from the chamber. One member of the Vanguard movement chained himself to one of the chairs and five police officers were injured as they tried to restore order.

UK general election, February 1974

Support for the power-sharing institutions was further weakened when the British prime minister Edward Heath called a general election for February 1974. Of the 12 Westminster seats for Northern Ireland constituencies, unionist candidates opposed to Sunningdale won 11 seats and the remaining seat was won by the SDLP. The popular slogan **'Dublin is just a Sunningdale away'** helped to persuade unionist voters that the agreement was the first step on the path to Irish unity. The result clearly indicated the outright rejection of power-sharing institutions and the Council of Ireland by the unionist community.

Merlyn Rees becomes secretary of state

The Labour party won the most seats in the election in Britain and took office as a minority government. Harold Wilson became prime minister and appointed Merlyn Rees as secretary of state for Northern Ireland. Wilson visited Northern Ireland in April 1974 to show his support for the power-sharing institutions. At this point, however, opposition to the assembly and executive was growing in strength. A strike organised by loyalist workers the following month eventually resulted in the collapse of the Sunningdale Agreement.

An anti-Sunningdale election poster used during the general election in 1974

Merlyn Rees, secretary of state for Northern Ireland in Harold Wilson's Labour government

How did the Ulster Workers' Council strike of May 1974 help cause the collapse of the Sunningdale Agreement?

Ulster Workers' Council

The **Ulster Workers' Council** (UWC) was an organisation of loyalist workers drawn from traditionally Protestant industries – such as ship building and electricity supply – that formed in 1969. Following the Sunningdale Agreement they began to advocate strike action as a way of bringing down the assembly and executive. Anti-Sunningdale unionist leaders **Ian Paisley**, **Harry West** and **William Craig** were brought on to the UWC committee coordinating the strike action. **Andy Tyrie**, a full-time officer with the paramilitary organisation the UDA, was also brought on to the committee. With the result of the general election showing that a majority of unionists were opposed to Sunningdale, the UWC felt justified in beginning all-out strike action.

Ulster Workers' Council strike, May 1974

In the assembly on 14 May 1974, a vote calling for the rejection of the Sunningdale Agreement was defeated. That evening **Harry Murray**, chairperson of the UWC, announced that a workers' strike would begin the next day.

Striking workers queue outside a dole office during the Ulster Workers' Council strike

On the morning of Wednesday, 15 May support for the UWC strike was limited. The **Chamber of Commerce** in Belfast reported that 90% of their workforce had turned up for work. The situation changed when Tyrie and the UDA began to get involved in enforcing the strike. Their tactics included shouting abuse at workers as they walked to factories, hijacking buses to stop workers from getting to their jobs, putting up roadblocks to physically stop workers from going to their jobs and threatening business owners that their premises would be petrol bombed if they remained open. The use of intimidation meant that by Wednesday evening the majority of factories and businesses in Belfast had shut down. The strike gradually spread across unionist areas of Northern Ireland and continued for two weeks.

A particularly effective tactic used by the UWC was the control of power stations by loyalists. This resulted in a reduction of electricity generation to 60% of the normal supply, forcing many factories to stop production and businesses to shut down. As **power blackouts** occurred on a daily basis the situation became critical in hospitals, farms and homes.

During the strike one of the worst incidents of the Troubles occurred on 17 May when the loyalist Ulster Volunteer Force detonated a series of car bombs in Dublin and Monaghan, killing 33 people and injuring several hundred.

The scene of the explosion on Talbot Street in Dublin, 17 May 1974

Response to the strike

The **British Army** was reluctant to take action against the striking workers. They considered their role as dealing with terrorism and that protest action such as a strike should be dealt with by the RUC. They also argued that they did not have the technical skills necessary to operate power stations. By the second week, the **commanding officer in Northern Ireland** believed that the strike was so widespread that he did not have enough troops to break it.

For Brian Faulkner, the actions of the striking workers undermined the authority of the executive. He could not take action as security powers remained in the hands of Westminster. Harold Wilson and Merlyn Rees were reluctant to send in troops but as time went on Wilson became increasingly frustrated by the situation.

On 25 May, Wilson made a controversial television broadcast condemning the strike. In his address he referred to loyalists as '**thugs and bullies**' and accused them of '**sponging on Westminster and British democracy**' because of the amount of money the government was spending on Northern Ireland.

Collapse of the executive and the end of the strike

The Army began to take control of fuel supplies by giving out petrol at pumps but the UWC responded by escalating their protest. On the thirteenth day of the strike they announced a total shutdown of electricity supply. The situation had reached crisis point with widespread food shortages, gas shortages and the breakdown of the telephone system.

British Army soldiers surround a petrol station with barbed wire in order to take control of fuel supplies, during the strike

The farmers' demonstration outside Stormont turned into celebration when news comes through that the Executive had resigned

British prime minister, Harold Wilson

Faulkner suggested that the executive enter into negotiations with the UWC but this was not acceptable to either the SDLP ministers or Rees. On 28 May Faulkner and his Ulster Unionist Party ministers resigned from the executive. This resulted in the collapse of the executive. Hundreds of farmers with tractors and farm machinery were already gathered at Stormont at a UWC-organised protest. Their protest turned to celebration as more loyalists gathered outside the building to celebrate their victory in bringing down the power-sharing institutions.

The UWC called off the strike the following morning and the striking workers returned to work. At a British cabinet meeting that afternoon Wilson reinstated direct rule to Northern Ireland.

What was the impact of the collapse of the Sunningdale Agreement?

The negotiation of the power-sharing institutions and the Sunningdale Agreement had taken over a year. The collapse of the executive was seen as a major blow in finding a political solution to the conflict in Northern Ireland.

There was widespread condemnation in Britain and Ireland that a strike organised by unelected individuals had the power to bring down democratically elected institutions.

The **Northern Ireland Constitutional Convention** was established in May 1975 but it was unsuccessful in finding a political solution as the majority of unionist members were against power-sharing.

The Sunningdale Agreement did not lead to a decrease in violence and the bombing campaigns of loyalist and republican paramilitaries continued after the collapse of the agreement.

British government saw 'the Irish dimension' as the main reason for the downfall of the Sunningdale Agreement. For some time afterwards, the British government shifted focus away from the developing north–south relations.

Although the Sunningdale Agreement failed, many of the ideas

Supporters of the UWC strike at a rally at Stormont to celebrate the collapse of the Executive. William Craig is in the centre of the image and Andy Tyrie is to Craig's right

contained in the document formed the basis of later agreements relating to Northern Ireland. The **Good Friday (Belfast) Agreement (1998)** included an assembly, power-sharing executive and Council of Ireland as part of the settlement.

REVIEW QUESTIONS

1	What groups came together to form the United Ulster Unionists Council?
2	Describe the response to the Sunningdale Agreement within the nationalist community.
3	What happened at a meeting of the Ulster Unionist Council on 4 January 1974?
4	What was the result of the Westminster general election in Northern Ireland in February 1974?
5	Explain in your own words the message behind the unionist slogan 'Dublin is just a Sunningdale away'.
6	Who was appointed secretary of state for Northern Ireland following the general election?
7	What was the Ulster Workers' Council and why did they feel justified in beginning strike action?
8	What tactics were used by Tyrie and the UDA to enforce the strike?
9	What tactic of the UWC was particularly effective?
10	Why was the Army reluctant to intervene in the strike?
11	Why was Harold Wilson's television address on 25 May seen as insensitive?
12	What caused the collapse of the Northern Ireland executive on 28 May?

EXAMINE THE SOURCES

Source 1

Disorder at a meeting of the Northern Ireland assembly, 22 January 1974

Immediately after prayers, Major Hall Thompson raised a point of order concerning the misappropriation [taking without permission] of seats reserved for Members of the Executive. Mr Speaker ordered Members occupying these seats to vacate them. Dr [Ian] Paisley, who was one of the Members concerned rose on a point of order, which Mr Speaker refused to accept. At this, a number of Members rose to protest and uproar commenced. Among other disorders which I noticed at this time, I particularly remember:-

(a) Mr Beattie snatching the mace [a metal staff representing royal authority in a parliament] from the table, passing it to another Member (I think Mr James Craig) who tossed it to another Member, when it was shortly afterward intercepted by one of the Doorkeepers who brought it to me. I gave directions that it was to be placed in safe custody, until such time as I decided it could safely be restored to the table.

(b) Professor Lindsay jumping on the table and carrying on, what I can only describe as a "war dance" on the table, shouting the while to press and visitors' galleries.

Source: PRONI Public Records ANI/10/110 Note on proceedings of the Northern Ireland assembly, 22 January 1974 (available on CAIN website)

(a) What point of order was raised following prayers?

(b) What did Ian Paisley refuse to do when ordered?

(c) What did Mr Beattie do with the mace?

(d) Describe the behaviour of Professor Lindsay.

(e) Based on your knowledge of this period, what was the Northern Ireland assembly and how was it formed?

(f) Based on the evidence in this account, do you think that the authority of the assembly was under threat? Explain your answer using evidence from the text.

Source 2

This cartoon was published shortly after British prime minister Harold Wilson's controversial television address and shows Wilson receiving a number of phone calls from a variety of people with different interests in Northern Ireland.

Cartoon published in *The Sun* newspaper during the Ulster Workers' Council strike, 27 May 1974

Source: Nina Kent

(a) Identify by name the following people:
  (i) The caller asking Wilson what he is doing about the Workers' Council
  (ii) The caller asking Wilson what he is doing about the north
  (iii) The caller asking Wilson what he is doing about the south.
(b) What message, do you think, is the cartoonist trying to convey about the situation Wilson found himself in, in May 1974?

DOCUMENTS-BASED QUESTIONS

The following are three documents-based questions. Use them to practise for your exam.

Question 1 (Higher Level)

Study the two sources below and answer the questions that follow.

Document A

Statement of Brian Faulkner, leader of the Ulster Unionist Party, at the opening of the Sunningdale conference 6 December 1973.

> We see this conference as concerned with North/South relations and how they can be improved. One thing is absolutely essential if the majority in Northern Ireland is to have any confidence in the future, that is that the Republic must make clear its acceptance of the right of the people of Northern Ireland to order their own affairs.
>
> We have a difficult path to tread. Power-sharing is not yet widely accepted by our fellow citizens. Even to conceive of a Council of Ireland is 100 times more difficult for unionists (with a small u) to accept than a power-sharing executive. All unionists (with a small u) fear that in a Council of Ireland there may be hidden a halfway house to a united Ireland. Therefore the recognition of our right to self-determination is of paramount importance. Only if this is accepted can any other form of co-operation between north/south begin.
>
> *Source:* National Archives of Ireland, Public Records TSCH 2004/21/627 (available on CAIN website)

Document B

Austin Currie, a member of the SDLP delegation at the Sunningdale conference, explains why the Council of Ireland was significant for his party.

> From the SDLP point of view, we hoped that in the Council of Ireland, even with its limitations [restrictions], we had helped to create something which, over a period of time, could develop and evolve to ensure a more united island, on an agreed basis. We felt sure that the opportunity to work together, North and South, in tackling common problems would create a situation where such common activity for mutual advantage would be taken for granted, and would be built upon at all levels. We did not see the Council as a threat to the fundamental interests of unionists. The Status Declaration by the Irish government, supported fully by the SDLP, enshrined unionist consent to change in the constitutional position and besides, decisions taken by the Council of Ministers had to be unanimous [supported by everyone].
>
> *Source:* Austin Currie, *All Hell Will Break Loose* (Dublin: O'Brien Press, 2004), pp. 234–235

1 Comprehension

(a) According to document A, what was essential for the majority in Northern Ireland to have any confidence in the future?

(b) In document A, why do unionists fear a Council of Ireland?

(c) In document B, how might the Council of Ireland develop and evolve over time?

(d) According to document B, what would the Council of Ireland not threaten?

2 Comparison

(a) Does the evidence in document B support the contention in document A that the Council of Ireland might eventually lead to a united Ireland? Explain your answer using evidence from both documents.

(b) From the evidence in both documents, do you think that a Council of Ireland was likely to be successful? Give reasons for your answer.

3 Criticism

(a) Based on your knowledge of the period and the evidence in document A, why was it of 'paramount importance' to unionists that the Irish government recognise the right to self-determination of the people of Northern Ireland?

(b) What are the strengths and weaknesses of document B as a historical source?

4 Contextualisation

What were the main elements of the Sunningdale Agreement, 1973 and why was it significant?

Question 2 (Ordinary Level, 2010)

Study the two sources below and answer the questions that follow.

Document A

Journalist Robert Fisk describes the first day of the Ulster Workers' Council strike, 15 May 1974.

By midday, intimidation was beginning to reach epic proportions. At Larne ... masked UDA men in camouflage jackets and carrying heavy wooden clubs roamed the streets around the docks. Wearing UDA insignia [badges], they called methodically at every shop in the town and ordered their owners to close down. Several uniformed men hijacked cars and lorries and placed them across the harbour roads ... Larne was effectively under siege but no attempt was made by the police to remove the road-blocks and no attempt was made by the Army ... to order the UDA off the streets. Perhaps the most spectacular mass intimidation, however, occurred at Harland and Wolff's where about 8,000 shipyard manual workers were invited to hear loyalist speeches during their lunch break. They did not get the address they expected, however, because unnamed speakers announced that any cars still in the employees' car park at two o'clock that afternoon would be burnt. The 8,000 left immediately and the yard closed down.

Source: Robert Fisk, The Point of No Return: the Strike which broke the British in Ulster (London: Times Books, 1975), p. 59

Document B

Extract from a television broadcast by Prime Minister Harold Wilson on the Ulster Workers' Council strike, 25 May 1974.

Today the law is being set aside. [...] Those who are now challenging constitutional authority are denying the fundamental right of every man and woman the right to work. They have decided, without having been elected by a single vote, who shall work in Northern Ireland and who shall not. They seek to allocate food, to decide who shall eat and who shall not. By their action, children are prevented from going to school, essential services are in peril. The payment of social security benefits is reduced to chaos through interference with the methods of payment. By their use of force and intimidation they have condemned hundreds of thousands of workers to involuntary unemployment. What they do not realise – what I hope that they do not realise – is how far they may be imperilling the jobs of Northern Ireland for years to come. ... We recognise that behind this situation lie many genuine and deeply held fears. I have to say that these fears are unfounded: that they are being deliberately fostered by people in search of power.

Source: The British National Archives (available on CAIN website)

1 Comprehension

(a) According to document A, what action was carried out by 'several uniformed men'?

(b) In document A, how many shipyard workers were invited to hear loyalist speeches?

(c) According to document A, how did 'unnamed speakers' threaten employees of Harland and Wolff?

(d) According to document B, what impact has the strike had on children?

(e) According to document B, what do those organising the strike not realise?

2 Comparison

(a) Do both documents agree that tactics of intimidation were being used to enforce the strike?

(b) Which document, A or B, would be more valuable to the historian? Give a reason for your answer.

3 Criticism

(a) Based on the evidence in document A, were the UDA able to enforce the strike with ease? Support your answer with reference to the document.

(b) Why is document B a primary source? Give a reason for your answer.

4 Contextualisation

What was the Sunningdale Agreement and why did most Unionists oppose it?

Question 3 (Higher Level, 2010)

Study the two sources below and answer the questions that follow.

Document A

Brian Faulkner, chief executive of the power-sharing executive, brought about by the Sunningdale Agreement, recalls the Ulster Workers' Council strike.

On Monday morning, 20 May 1974, I was told by the police that there were so many barricades on roads between my home and Stormont that I would have to be flown in by helicopter. As we travelled across County Down I could see beneath me the evidence of para-military activity.

Even at Stormont, as we came in to land, I could see a barricade within sight of Merlyn Rees' office. I went in to the Secretary of State (Rees) and demanded, angrily, that something be done to remove all the barricades; but he insisted, at first, that the security forces had the problem under control and that the roads were, in general, clear.

I ended the argument by taking him to the window and pointing to the barricade at Dundonald House; and, in agitation, he turned to instruct his officials to have it cleared. Shortly afterwards a bulldozer arrived and pushed the obstruction aside; but, in an hour or so, it was up again at the same spot.

Source: Edited extract from Brian Faulkner, *Memoirs of a Statesman* (London: Weidenfeld & Nicolson, 1978)

Document B

Merlyn Rees, the British government's secretary of state for Northern Ireland, writes of that time.

Our very position in the province was in question. I had personally been warned of an assassination attempt; and I, with my small Northern Ireland British staff, found it difficult to travel the roads. We had tried 'choppering' [travelling by helicopter] from the Culloden Hotel, but working from there at night, in inadequate quarters, had been proving difficult.

We, therefore, decided to camp in the Speaker's House at Stormont. The conditions were elementary – camp beds, tinned food – and the atmosphere was reminiscent of periods in my war service. We were isolated, working long hours, and I do not think Westminster realised how difficult that time was for us. Every report we received showed the deteriorating situation. Effective administration was in the hands of the strikers.

Source: Edited extract from Merlyn Rees, *Northern Ireland: A Personal Perspective* (London: Methuen, 1985)

1 Comprehension

(a) According to document A, why did Brian Faulkner travel to Stormont by helicopter?

(b) According to document A, what sort of activity did Faulkner see on the ground?

(c) According to document A, what demand did Faulkner make in the secretary of state's office?

(d) In document B, what complaint did Merlyn Rees have against the British government?

2 Comparison

(a) Do the documents support the claim, made by Rees in document A, that the authorities were in control of security? Explain your answer, referring to both documents.

(b) From the evidence of the documents, who showed better leadership, Faulkner or Rees? Give reasons for your answer.

3 Criticism

(a) Should a historian accept document A as a reliable source? Give reasons for your answer.

(b) What are the strengths and weaknesses of document B as a historical source?

4 Contextualisation

What were the difficulties associated with implementing the Sunningdale Agreement?

Terence O'Neill (1914–1990)

Terence O'Neill was born in London in 1914. Just two months after he was born, his father, Arthur O'Neill (the unionist MP for mid-Antrim), died in action during the First World War. Terence spent his childhood summer holidays in the family's ancestral home of **Shane's Castle**, Co. Antrim. He was educated at the prestigious **Eton College** in Berkshire, England.

O'Neill joined the **Irish Guards** during the Second World War and in 1944 he took part in the Allied invasion of western Europe, advancing across Belgium and Holland. He suffered personal tragedy during the war with two of his brothers and a close friend killed in action.

After the war O'Neill and his young family settled in Co. Antrim. In November 1946 he was selected by the Ulster Unionist Party to run in the Bannside constituency and was elected unopposed to the Stormont parliament.

O'Neill was promoted quickly from the position of backbencher, becoming parliamentary secretary to the minister of health in 1948. In April 1956, age 42, he was appointed **minister of home affairs** and six months later was made **minister of finance**.

As minister of finance O'Neill had to deal with a worsening economic situation. The postwar decline of industries such as shipbuilding, linen and aircraft manufacture resulted in high rates of unemployment in Northern Ireland. O'Neill continued the traditional Ulster Unionist Party policy of seeking assistance from the British government to boost employment in the existing industries in Northern Ireland.

A turning point came with the publication of the **Hall Report** in 1962. The report was critical of the Northern Ireland government's economic policy and recommended that the government should try to attract foreign investors to set up factories and businesses in Northern Ireland. The negative reaction to the report was a factor that contributed to the resignation of **Basil Brooke (Lord Brookeborough)** as prime minister in February 1963.

O'Neill was chosen as the new leader of the Ulster Unionist Party and, therefore, prime minister by the governor of Northern Ireland. On taking office his stated aim was to 'transform Ulster' and he set about achieving this by improving the relationship between the unionist and nationalist communities and introducing economic reforms.

In terms of community relations, O'Neill tried to build bridges between Catholics and Protestants. He regularly visited Catholic schools and convents and was photographed shaking hands with priests. He did not, however, introduce any specific policy or legislation to end the practices that discriminated against Catholics and that would later lead to the growth of the **civil rights movement**.

Many of his efforts to reach out to the nationalist community were met with strong opposition from within the unionist movement. **Ian Paisley's** slogan 'O'Neill must go' became popular among members on the more extreme wing of the party who wanted to oust O'Neill.

A significant development in healing the divide between the north and south of Ireland was O'Neill's meetings with the Taoiseach, **Seán Lemass**, in 1965. Lemass visited Stormont in January and O'Neill made a return visit to Dublin in February. The men discussed matters of mutual interest such as tourism but avoided discussing controversial topics.

O'Neill was aware of the success of economic planning that had taken place in the Republic of Ireland in the late 1950s. The recommendations of the *First Programme for Economic Expansion* (1958) written by **T.K. Whitaker**, a civil servant at the department of finance, led to an increase in economic growth and foreign firms locating their factories in Ireland. Economic plans and reports were commissioned under O'Neill's government, such as:

- **Matthew Plan (1962):** recommended large-scale house building and the creation of a new city to restrict the growth of Belfast
- **Wilson Plan (1964):** identified specific areas of Northern Ireland to be targeted for economic development; proposed new infrastructure, in particular the building of motorways; the provision of grants and tax allowances to attract foreign firms to set up business in Northern Ireland
- **Lockwood Report:** recommended that Northern Ireland should have a second university and that the second university be located at **Coleraine**.

In the O'Neill years a number of foreign firms – such as **Grundig** and **Goodyear** – set up in Northern Ireland and there was a small increase in employment.

The Lockwood Report caused a great deal of controversy for O'Neill, with residents of Derry, which had a majority Catholic population, outraged that their city was overlooked as a location for a second university. O'Neill met with representatives of the **University for Derry Committee**, who tried to persuade him of the economic need for a university in the north-west region. O'Neill seems to have been more swayed by a secret meeting with unionists from Derry, who were concerned that a second university would disrupt the delicate system of **gerrymandering** in the city. In a vote on the recommendations of the Lockwood Committee, O'Neill **applied the whip**, forcing members of the Unionist Party to vote in favour of the report's findings.

Dealing with the demands of the **Northern Ireland Civil Rights Association (NICRA)** – to end practices that discriminated against Catholics in the areas of housing, voting and employment – was the greatest challenge of O'Neill's political career. A civil rights march in Derry on 5 October 1968 ended in violent clashes between the RUC and protestors. Images of the violence were broadcast around the world.

Under pressure from British prime minister **Harold Wilson** and in spite of strong opposition from cabinet members such as **William Craig** and **Brian Faulkner**, in November 1968 O'Neill introduced a **five-point plan** of reforms to deal with the concerns of the civil rights movement. In December he made a television address to the people of Northern Ireland, where he declared that '**Ulster stands at the crossroads**', on the brink of a descent into violence unless the civil rights protestors and their loyalist opponents showed restraint.

In spite of O'Neill's plea, violence continued to escalate in January 1969, when a group of loyalists attacked a march organised by the civil rights group **People's Democracy** at Burntollet Bridge. O'Neill came under increasing pressure from within his own cabinet. His decision to set up the **Cameron Commission** to investigate the disturbances at civil rights marches led to the resignation of Faulkner.

O'Neill decided to call a snap general election to face down growing opposition. The election was a clear victory for O'Neill: 27 of the 39 unionists elected supported his policies. However, there was also evidence of support weakening: Paisley ran against O'Neill in his Bannside constituency and lost out to him by just 1,414 votes.

On the return of the Stormont parliament, O'Neill continued to lose support from within his own party. The breaking point came when in April 1969 O'Neill agreed to introduce 'one man, one vote', allowing a universal right to vote in local elections. The decision prompted the resignation from cabinet of his cousin **James Chichester-Clark**. The reform was passed by a narrow margin by the Ulster Unionist Party but O'Neill sensed he was losing support rapidly. He announced his resignation on 28 April 1969.

O'Neill was replaced as prime minister by Chichester-Clark. He resigned his seat in Stormont in 1970 and was given a life peerage in the **House of Lords**.

Patricia McCluskey (1914–2010) and Conn McCluskey (1915–2013)

Patricia McCluskey (née McShane) was born in Portadown, Co. Armagh in 1914. She emigrated to Scotland where she worked as a home economics teacher. Conn McCluskey was born in Warrenpoint, Co. Down in 1915. He was educated at Blackrock College in Dublin and studied medicine in UCD.

Conn and Patricia met when Patricia was home on holidays. The couple married and eventually settled in the town of **Dungannon**, Co. Tyrone, where Conn set up a general medical practice.

Through Conn's work as a local doctor, the couple became aware of problems with housing in the town. Much of the housing in Dungannon was in poor condition and there were problems with overcrowding. Conn McCluskey learned of one case where a family of ten shared a one-room bedsit. Seven other families all inhabited one-room bedsits in the same building.

The McCluskeys were also concerned about how local authority housing was allocated in the town. In 1963, the population of Dungannon was about 7,000 people and there was a slight majority of Catholic residents. However, the system of **gerrymandering** ensured that unionist control of the town's council was almost guaranteed.

As housing was allocated to those who applied for it by the local councillors, it was alleged that unionist councillors favoured applications from Protestant families. Only **ratepayers** (householders) were allowed to vote in local elections. Therefore, it was not in the interests of unionist councillors to allocate houses to Catholics, as an increase in the number of Catholic voters could result in unionists losing power.

In 1963, Conn and Patricia were founding members of the **Homeless Citizens League**. Members of the league organised a picket outside the offices of the town council. Protestant families were moving out of temporary homes into newly built council houses. The league protested against the refusal of the council to give the empty temporary homes to Catholic families.

The protest gained widespread publicity and in 1964 Patricia was elected to the town council. Conn and Patricia saw the need to provide evidence in order to back up claims of discrimination against Catholics in the allocation of housing. To this end they set up the **Campaign for Social Justice** to investigate claims of discrimination in cases across Northern Ireland. Much of the evidence they uncovered was published in the pamphlet ***The Plain Truth*** (1964).

The Plain Truth documented examples of discrimination against Catholics in Derry, Enniskillen, Lurgan and Dungannon in the areas of voting, employment and housing. In Derry, for instance, the Campaign for Social Justice found that of 100 houses built by Derry Corporation on Academy Road in the city, only two were let to Catholic families. A case of Protestant control of local government employment in Enniskillen was outlined, where of the 76 local government positions in the town, only three of these positions were held by Catholics.

The work of the McCluskeys contributed to the rise of the civil rights movement. When the **Northern Ireland Civil Rights Association** formed in 1967, Conn was elected vice chairman. In June 1969, Campaign for Social Justice published a second edition of *The Plain Truth*, which contained an expanded account of discrimination against Catholics in Northern Ireland.

Conn continued to work as a doctor in Dungannon for the decades during the Troubles and the couple lived in Dublin during their retirement.

Bernadette Devlin (*b.* 1947)

Bernadette Devlin was born in Cookstown, Co. Tyrone. Her father could not get work in Northern Ireland and travelled regularly to England to find employment. At the age of 46 he died of a heart attack, after which Devlin's family survived mostly on welfare payments.

Devlin benefited from the **Education Act** (1947) which allowed her a grammar school education at **St Patrick's Academy, Dungannon** and she received a scholarship to study psychology at **Queen's University Belfast**.

Her time at Queen's coincided with the rise of the **civil rights movement** in the late 1960s. Devlin possessed a strong sense of **social justice** and was motivated to protest against the key civil rights issues of gerrymandering and discrimination in the allocation of housing and jobs.

She attended the first civil rights march from Coalisland to Dungannon on 24 August 1968. Like the other marchers she was prevented from entering Dungannon by a police cordon outside the town. On 5 October 1968 she attended a civil rights march in Derry, where she witnessed protestors being attacked by police.

Devlin returned to university and she and her fellow students organised a march from Queen's to Belfast City Hall on 9 October 1968. They were prevented from getting to City Hall via Shaftesbury Square by loyalist protestors. That night, along with other students and lecturers at the university, Devlin became a founding member of **People's Democracy**. Like the **Northern Ireland Civil Rights Association**, People's Democracy wanted to end practices that discriminated against Catholics but overall were more radical and **socialist** in their viewpoint.

Both Devlin and **People's Democracy** came to public attention in January 1969, when they organised a march from Belfast to Derry. On the fourth day of the march, at **Burntollet Bridge**, the marchers were ambushed by a group of loyalists and Devlin was struck by a wooden plank with nails sticking out of it.

Devlin was just 21 years old when she was elected MP to the **Westminster parliament** in a by-election in the mid-Ulster constituency in April 1969. She made her maiden speech on the same day as she took her seat in the House of Commons. Her attack on the Ulster Unionist Party and its policies was widely covered in the British press.

During the rioting in Derry in August 1969, Devlin was in the Bogside, instructing residents in how to guard the barricades. The following December she was sentenced to six months in prison for inciting violence and obstructing police during the rioting but was released on bail.

Devlin witnessed the events of **Bloody Sunday** in Derry in January 1972. During a sitting of the House of Commons she slapped the face of home secretary **Reginald Maudling** when he claimed that British soldiers had fired on civilians in self-defence.

Devlin lost her seat in the 1974 general election. She continued to be involved in socialist politics and was a founder member of the **Irish Republican Socialist Party** in 1974. She was unsuccessful in her attempts to run for election to the European Parliament (1979) and to Dáil Éireann (February and December 1982). In January 1981 she survived an assassination attempt by the **Ulster Defence Association (UDA)** when she was shot nine times in her home.

John Hume (1937-2020)

John Hume was born in Derry in 1937 and grew up in the Catholic **Bogside** area of the city. His father was unemployed from the time Hume was eight years old and his mother worked part-time in local shirt factories.

Hume was part of the first generation of children from working-class families to benefit from the introduction of the **welfare state** in Northern Ireland after the Second World War. The **Education Act** (1947) enabled Hume to obtain a grammar school education without having to pay fees. He went on to study history and French at **Maynooth University**.

In his early career he was involved in setting up **Derry Credit Union** and at the young age of 27 he was president of the **Credit Union League of Ireland**. He also set up a salmon-smoking enterprise in the city.

Hume first became active in politics in 1965, when the controversial **Lockwood Report** overlooked Derry and recommended that a second university for Northern Ireland be established in Coleraine. Hume, like others in Derry, regarded the decision as further evidence of an unofficial government policy of neglecting the majority Catholic north-west region. Hume was a founder member of the **University for Derry Action Committee**, which included representatives from both the unionist and nationalist communities. He organised a **motorcade** to travel from Derry to Stormont on 18 February 1965; approximately 2,000 vehicles took part in the protest. Hume was part of a delegation that met with prime minister **Terence O'Neill** and pleaded with him to locate the university in Derry. However, the campaign failed in its efforts to overturn the Lockwood decision.

Growing up as a Catholic in a working-class area of Derry, Hume was acutely aware of issues affecting his community, in particular in the area of housing. Problems with overcrowding and the failure of **Derry Corporation** to provide new housing in nationalist areas prompted Hume and others to take action themselves. Hume formed a **housing association** in an attempt to raise funds to buy land and build houses.

Frustration with the housing situation and other issues such as **gerrymandering** and employment discrimination spilled over in 1968 when controversial civil rights marches took place. Following the violent clashes between marchers and the RUC that occurred during a march in Derry in October 1968, the **Derry Citizens' Action Committee** was formed, with Hume as its vice-chair.

Hume began to realise that there were limits to the extent that citizen action groups could bring about change. He believed that in order to press for the introduction of real reforms he needed to become directly involved in politics. In 1969 he ran for election as an independent candidate to the Stormont parliament and defeated the sitting Nationalist Party MP **Eddie McAteer**. The following year, Hume was a founding member of the **Social, Democratic and Labour Party (SDLP)**.

Like his fellow members of the SDLP, Hume was in favour of using only peaceful means to resolve conflict. He favoured the use of **passive resistance** as a form of protest. On 22 January 1972, Hume led a peaceful march against internment along **Magilligan Strand**, the location of an internment camp. Hume and the marchers were confronted by British soldiers who fired rubber bullets at the crowd. The following Sunday became known as **Bloody Sunday**, when 14 unarmed civilians died having been shot by British soldiers during an anti-internment protest march in Derry. Hume had not taken part in the march as he anticipated the violence that would take place that day.

As a member of the SDLP, Hume took part in the negotiations that led to the **Sunningdale Agreement** in 1973. Hume believed that **power-sharing** between unionists and nationalists and the introduction of a **Council of Ireland** to promote good north–south relations would provide a long-term solution to the conflict in Northern Ireland.

Hume was appointed **minister of commerce** in the short-lived **executive** that began functioning in January 1974. In May 1974 a workers' strike brought Northern Ireland to a standstill. The executive collapsed when Hume and other members of the SDLP refused to enter into talks with the organisers of the strike, the **Ulster Workers' Council**.

In spite of the collapse of the institutions set up under the Sunningdale Agreement, Hume continued to search for a political solution to the conflict that would bring peace. As a politician he was outward-looking and saw the potential in forming relationships with Irish-American politicians who might assist with the search for peace. From 1972 he was in regular contact with the American senator **Ted Kennedy**. In 1973, Northern Ireland, as part of the United Kingdom, became a member of the **European Economic Union (EEC)**. In 1979 Hume was elected as **MEP** to the **European Parliament** where he advocated for the EEC to provide economic assistance to Northern Ireland.

That same year, Hume replaced **Gerry Fitt** as leader of the SDLP. In 1983 he was elected for the Westminster constituency of **Foyle**. Hume was an enthusiastic supporter of the **New Ireland Forum**, established in 1983 by the Irish Taoiseach, **Garret FitzGerald**. FitzGerald worked closely with Hume during the forum to come up with a number of proposals, which included: a **united**

Ireland, with a single government for the island of Ireland; a **federal Ireland**, where Northern Ireland would have its own parliament within a united Ireland and a proposal for the **joint government** of Northern Ireland by London and Dublin.

Although the British prime minister **Margaret Thatcher** rejected the proposals of the New Ireland Forum, she was willing to pursue some form of political solution to the conflict. In 1985 the **Anglo-Irish Agreement** was signed at Hillsborough Castle, which accepted the principle that there would be no unity in Ireland without the consent of the majority in Northern Ireland and that there would be regular intergovernmental conferences between north and south. Hume welcomed the agreement and considered that it provided a framework in which a political solution could be found.

Hume felt that no lasting solution would be arrived at without the involvement of **Sinn Féin** and the **Provisional IRA** in negotiations. In 1988 Hume held a series of secret talks with the president of Sinn Féin, Gerry Adams, at **Clonard Monastery** in west Belfast. When news of the discussions became public, Hume received a lot of criticism for negotiating with terrorists. The talks also experienced setbacks with continuing IRA violence during this period.

In December 1993, prime minister **John Major** and Taoiseach **Albert Reynolds** announced the **Downing Street Declaration**. Many of the principles agreed in the declaration were the result of the talks that had taken place between Gerry Adams and John Hume. One aspect of the declaration was that those associated with republican and loyalist violence could take part in negotiations if they gave up violence. The following year both the IRA and loyalist paramilitaries declared ceasefires.

John Hume is seen as one of the main instigators of the peace process that eventually resulted in the **Good Friday Agreement** in 1998. That same year his contribution to peace-making was acknowledged when he was awarded the **Nobel Peace Prize** alongside Ulster Unionist Party leader **David Trimble**.

Brian Faulkner (1921–1977)

Brian Faulkner was born into a **Presbyterian** family in Co. Down and educated at **St Columba's College** in Dublin. His father, James, established a successful shirt-making factory in Belfast.

Shortly after Faulkner began studying law at **Queen's University Belfast**, the Second World War broke out. He left his studies to assist his father and brother in running the family business. Unlike many of his future political colleagues, Faulkner did not serve in the forces during the war.

Faulkner became involved in politics after the war. He started the **Young Unionist** movement in an attempt to modernise the way the **Ulster Unionist Party** was organised. In 1949, with the encouragement of **Terence O'Neill**, Faulkner ran for election as MP for the Northern Ireland parliament at Stormont and won the **East Down** constituency seat.

In 1959 Faulkner became **minister of home affairs** in the government of **Basil Brooke (Lord Brookeborough)**. He dealt swiftly with the IRA, threatening to introduce the death penalty following the murder of an RUC constable in Co. Armagh on 12 November 1961. A few months later the IRA issued a statement bringing an end to the **border campaign**.

When Lord Brookeborough resigned as prime minister in 1963, Faulkner was considered for leadership of the party, but his views were thought to be too hardline and his lack of service record during the Second World War went against him.

Terence O'Neill was appointed as the new leader of the party and became prime minister of Northern Ireland. He offered Faulkner the position of **minister of commerce**. Given Faulkner's background in running the family business he considered himself well-equipped to take on this role.

Faulkner became minister of commerce at a time when the policy of creating employment by attracting foreign firms to set up factories in Northern Ireland was gradually being introduced. He brought enthusiasm to the role and travelled widely to promote Northern Ireland as a location for international firms. During his time in office companies such as **Ford**, **Goodyear** and **Rolls Royce** established factories in Northern Ireland.

The relationship between Faulkner and O'Neill was a difficult one. In cabinet, Faulkner frequently opposed measures introduced by O'Neill, such as the economic programme known as the **Wilson Plan**. With the rise of the civil rights movement in 1968 and early 1969, Faulkner frequently clashed with O'Neill in cabinet. O'Neill attempted to address the protests of the civil rights marchers by introducing reforms while the marches were still ongoing. Faulkner, on the other hand, opposed the introduction of reforms until the civil unrest was brought under control.

In January 1969 O'Neill announced the setting up of the **Cameron Commission** to investigate the disturbances that had occurred during recent civil rights protests. Shortly afterwards, Faulkner resigned from cabinet in protest at this decision.

O'Neill resigned as prime minister in April 1969. Faulkner ran against **James Chichester-Clark** in the contest for leadership of the party and lost out to him by a single vote. He was appointed minister of development in Chichester-Clark's new cabinet. One of his areas of responsibility was housing and his task was to implement the reform introduced by O'Neill of allocating housing on a points system.

Chichester-Clark's time in office was short-lived. He struggled to deal with the sharp escalation in violence across Northern Ireland that occurred with the commencement of the marching season in the summer of 1969 and the growth of paramilitary organisations. He resigned as prime minister in March 1971.

Faulkner was seen as the logical choice to replace Chichester-Clark. In a vote of members of the parliamentary party, Faulkner defeated the hardline unionist **William Craig** to become leader of the Ulster Unionist Party and prime minister of Northern Ireland.

On coming to power, Faulkner attempted to ease the divisions within the Ulster Unionist Party by offering a cabinet position to **Harry West**, a hardline unionist who had been expelled from the party in 1969. He also tried to broaden the range of opinion in cabinet by appointing a member of the **Northern Ireland Labour Party**, **David Bleakley**, as minister of community relations. In June 1971, Faulkner announced that members of the opposition would be allowed to chair parliamentary committees. For the first time, members of the nationalist parties at Stormont would have the chance to influence government legislation.

In spite of his efforts to introduce reforms, Faulkner faced serious challenges from the outset of his premiership. Paramilitary violence escalated in the spring and summer of 1971. IRA bomb attacks became more frequent and widespread rioting broke out with the onset of the marching season. Faulkner urged the use of **internment**, a policy he had advocated for some time. Imprisonment without trial was introduced on 9 August 1971. The policy proved disastrous as the arrests were targeted at the nationalist community which had the unintended consequence of increasing membership of the IRA.

Another challenge faced by Faulkner was hardening opposition from within the wider unionist movement to the introduction of any measures that could be seen as making concessions to the nationalist community. Faulkner's policies were opposed by the extreme loyalist **Ian Paisley**. In March 1972 **William Craig** and other members of the Ulster Unionist Party formed the **Vanguard movement**, advocating a semi-independent Ulster.

The events of **Bloody Sunday**, when British Army paratroopers shot dead 14 unarmed civilians on the streets of Derry on 30 January 1972, persuaded the British government that Faulkner's government could no longer control the security situation in Northern Ireland. Faulkner strongly opposed the British government's intention to take control of all security matters and warned of dire consequences if direct rule was introduced.

Nonetheless, on 24 March 1972 British prime minister Ted Heath announced that the Stormont parliament would no longer function and Northern Ireland would be governed from Westminster. **William Whitelaw** was appointed by Heath to the new role of **secretary of state for Northern Ireland**. Faulkner remained leader of the Ulster Unionist Party but was no longer prime minister of Northern Ireland.

In March 1973 the British government published the white paper ***Northern Ireland: constitutional proposals***, which contained a framework for a new system of government. It proposed institutions such as an **assembly** elected by proportional representation and an **executive** where power would be shared between nationalist and unionist politicians. Faulkner described the proposals as 'constructive'.

Elections to the new assembly were held in June 1973. Candidates who supported Faulkner and the power-sharing proposals won 24 seats but unionist candidates against power-sharing won 26 seats. Negotiations to form the power-sharing executive took place in November 1973 and Faulkner succeeded in securing 6 of the 11 seats on the executive for the Ulster Unionist Party. Faulkner himself would have the role of **chief executive**.

Faulkner led the Ulster Unionist Party delegation during the Sunningdale negotiations in December 1973. These negotiations aimed to find agreement on how the proposed **Council of Ireland** would function. The purpose of the Council of Ireland was to give the Republic of Ireland a say in the affairs of Northern Ireland. It was strongly opposed by many unionists, in particular the Vanguard wing of the Ulster Unionist Party.

With the **Sunningdale Agreement**, Faulkner believed that he had negotiated a Council of Ireland in which the government of the Republic of Ireland would have limited influence over policies relating to Northern Ireland. He underestimated the opposition to the Council of Ireland within his own party. This soon became evident when the **Ulster Unionist Council** voted to reject the Sunningdale Agreement in January 1974, forcing Faulkner to resign as party leader.

Faulkner continued as chief executive but his position became increasingly untenable. A general election in February 1974 resulted in a humiliating defeat for Faulkner, when not a single candidate who supported the Sunningdale Agreement was elected.

The situation worsened with the outbreak of the **Ulster Workers' Council (UWC)** strike in May 1974. As the strike brought a widespread shut-down of services across Northern Ireland, it seemed as if extreme loyalist groups were more in control of Northern Ireland than Faulkner's executive. When the SDLP refused to allow the executive to negotiate with the UWC, Faulkner resigned, bringing about the collapse of the executive. Direct rule was reinstated in Northern Ireland.

Faulkner resigned from politics in 1976. The following year he died in a hunting accident at the age of 56.

Ian Paisley (1926–2014)

Ian Paisley, the son of a Baptist minister, was born in Armagh. His family could trace its origins to Scottish settlers who arrived in Ulster in the early 17th century. Paisley learned the skill of preaching at an evangelical school in Wales and was 20 years old when his father ordained him a minister. In 1951 Paisley established his own church, the **Free Presbyterian Church**.

Paisley was known for his strongly anti-Catholic views. He was militant in his opposition to **ecumenism**, a movement that encouraged a closer relationship between the Catholic and Protestant churches, both in Ireland and around the world. In June 1963, for example, Paisley strongly condemned the prime minister **Terence O'Neill** and other public figures for expressing sympathies on the death of **Pope John XXIII**.

Paisley's words often provoked violence. In 1964 he threatened to remove an Irish tricolour from a window of the headquarters of the **Republican Party** in Belfast if the authorities did not do so. The RUC's efforts to remove the flag led to clashes between the police and locals that descended into serious sectarian rioting across west Belfast.

Paisley's public profile continued to grow in the mid-1960s. He set up his own newspaper, the *Protestant Telegraph*, as a platform for his views. In 1965 he established the **Ulster Protestant Volunteers**, a **loyalist** group who were prepared to use force if necessary in a time of crisis. His extreme Protestant views were evident in 1966 when he led a protest to the **Presbyterian General Assembly** in Belfast and shouted insults at those who emerged from the building, including the governor of Northern Ireland and his wife. He was convicted of unlawful assembly and imprisoned in Crumlin Road gaol for three months.

Paisley opposed prime minister **Terence O'Neill's** efforts to reach out to the Catholic community in Northern Ireland. The day after Taoiseach **Seán Lemass** met with O'Neill in Belfast in February 1965, Paisley handed in a letter of protest to Stormont. During the era of the **civil rights movement** it was unsurprising that Paisley was bitterly opposed to any reforms proposed by O'Neill to address the demands of civil rights protestors.

Paisley believed that organisations such as the **Northern Ireland Civil Rights Association (NICRA)** were being controlled by the IRA. He arranged for **counter-demonstrations** to take place at civil rights marches. It was supporters of Paisley, led by his ally **Ronald Bunting**, that attacked marchers from the **People's Democracy** at **Burntollet Bridge** in January 1969.

In the February 1969 Stormont election Paisley challenged O'Neill in the **Bannside** constituency and lost by only 1,414 votes. In April 1970 he was elected to the Bannside seat left vacant by O'Neill following his resignation. Two months later Paisley was elected MP to Westminster for the **North Antrim** constituency. In 1971 he established the **Democratic Unionist Party (DUP)** which he remained the leader of until May 2008.

In protest at the **Sunningdale Agreement**, Paisley and the DUP joined the **United Ulster Unionist Council (UUUC)**, an umbrella group of anti-Sunningdale unionists. He was elected to Westminster as a UUUC candidate in 1974. Later that year, Paisley sat on the organising committee of the **Ulster Workers' Council strike**; the committee included members of the paramilitary organisation the **Ulster Defence Association (UDA)**.

Paisley was the central figure in organising another strike in May 1977 with a group called the **Ulster Unionist Action Council**. The strike was in protest at the policies of the secretary of state **Roy Mason** and the Labour government of **James Callaghan**. The action was met with the disapproval of the leader of the UUUC at Westminster, **James Molyneaux**. The strike failed to gain widespread support and collapsed within a few days.

Paisley's DUP generally came second to the **Ulster Unionist Party** in terms of votes. The popularity of the DUP increased throughout the 1970s and in 1979 two new DUP MPs were elected to Westminster and Paisley won a comfortable victory in his election as **MEP** to the **European Parliament**.

He was appalled by the **Anglo-Irish Agreement** in 1985. He accused prime minister **Margaret Thatcher** of treachery for negotiating with the Irish government. He held a huge rally of loyalist supporters at City Hall in Belfast on 23 November 1985. Paisley's cry of '**Never, Never, Never!**' was seen as symbolic of an unwillingness to compromise among many unionists.

As the peace process developed in the 1990s, Paisley took a hardline stance and would not participate in talks alongside **Sinn Féin**. He opposed the **Good Friday Agreement** in 1998 and support for the DUP increased in the years that followed the agreement. It was considered a remarkable turn of events when in 2006, as part of the **St Andrew's Agreement**, Paisley's DUP agreed to share power with **Sinn Féin** in a devolved government in Northern Ireland.

Gerry Adams
(*b.* 1948)

Gerry Adams was born in west Belfast, into a family that had a history of involvement in the **republican movement** in Ireland. As a teenager he left St Mary's Christian Brothers' School to become an apprentice barman.

Adams joined the **Northern Ireland Civil Rights Association** and took part in civil rights protests in the late 1960s. As the marches turned violent, Adams took part in the rioting that spread from Derry to Belfast in August 1969. He abandoned his apprenticeship as a barman and devoted himself to full-time involvement in the republican movement.

Following the introduction of internment, Adams was interned under the **Special Powers Act** in 1972 on the *HMS Maidstone* prison ship. An **IRA** ceasefire was negotiated in June 1972 and Adams was released from prison. He took part in talks in London between the British secretary of state **William Whitelaw** and **Provisional IRA** negotiators. The talks collapsed when Whitelaw could not meet the IRA demand for British withdrawal from Northern Ireland. The ceasefire ended on **Bloody Friday**, 21 July 1972, when the IRA detonated 20 bombs within 65 minutes in Belfast, killing nine people and seriously injuring 130 people.

In 1973 Adams was rearrested and interned at **Long Kesh** prison camp. While in prison Adams began to put forward what became known as '**the armalite and the ballot box**' strategy. Adams believed that the IRA were fighting what would be a 'long war' against British presence in Northern Ireland. In order to keep this effort going, the IRA would have to become involved in politics through the political wing of the organisation, **Sinn Féin**.

This strategy came to the fore in 1981 during the **hunger strikes**, when republican prisoners in the **Maze Prison** refused food in protest at the removal of **special category status** from convicted prisoners. Adams played an important role in the election of hunger striker **Bobby Sands** as an MP to the House of Commons in a by-election in Fermanagh.

In 1983, Adams was elected MP for West Belfast for the Sinn Féin party. He followed the party policy of **abstention** and did not take his seat in the Westminster parliament. The same year he was elected president of **Sinn Féin**. Under his leadership Sinn Féin took part in elections on both sides of the border and in 1986 Adams persuaded the party to end the policy of refusing to take their seats at **Dáil Éireann**.

Secret talks between Adams and the moderate nationalist leader **John Hume** took place at Clonard Monastery in Belfast in the late 1980s. The talks were seen as controversial but ultimately they enabled the **peace process** to happen by involving both republicans and more moderate nationalists in discussions.

Progress was damaged by continuing IRA violence, such as the **Shankill bombing** in October 1993 when an IRA bomb exploded prematurely, killing one of the IRA bombers, a UDA leader and nine Protestant civilians. Adams' decision to help carry the coffin of the deceased IRA bomber was widely condemned.

A significant breakthrough came with the declaration of an **IRA ceasefire** in 1994. This allowed Adams and other Sinn Féin members to take part in negotiations that resulted in the **Good Friday Agreement** in 1998. The same year, Adams was elected to the new Northern Ireland Assembly that was established as part of the Good Friday Agreement.

James Molyneaux (1920–2015)

James Molyneaux was born in Killead, Co. Antrim, where his family owned a small farm. On leaving school aged 15, Molyneaux helped his father set up a small poultry business. He joined the **Royal Air Force** in 1941 and during the Second World War he took part in the **D-Day landings** and the liberation of the **Bergen-Belsen concentration camp**.

On returning from war, Molyneaux resumed farm work and helped his uncle in running a printing business. Molyneaux was a member of his local **Orange Order** lodge and gradually became involved in politics through his local branch of the **Ulster Unionist Party**.

In 1970, Molyneaux was elected as an **MP** for South Antrim in the Westminster parliament. He was considered a hardline unionist and was selected as a candidate because it was felt he would appeal to grassroots voters. Many unionist voters were frustrated by how the Ulster Unionist Party were handling the growing situation of conflict in Northern Ireland.

In February 1972, Molyneaux joined the **Ulster Vanguard movement**, a group within the Ulster Unionist Party that were against introducing reforms that could be seen as making concessions to the nationalist community. He was opposed to the introduction of **direct rule** in 1972. However, he was also strongly against the establishment of a **power-sharing executive** in 1973. Over time, he came to support Northern Ireland being more closely integrated into the United Kingdom. This would avoid a situation where Northern Ireland would be jointly governed by nationalists and unionists.

In response to the **Sunningdale Agreement** in December 1973, an umbrella group called the **United Ulster Unionist Council (UUUC)** was formed to oppose power-sharing and the proposed **Council of Ireland**. Members included **Ian Paisley** and **Harry West**. In the **general election** of February 1974, Molyneaux was elected in South Antrim having run as a candidate for both the Ulster Unionist Party and the UUUC. Following the resignation of **Brian Faulkner**, Molyneaux put his name forward in the contest for the leadership of the Ulster Unionist Party but was defeated by Harry West.

At Westminster, Molyneaux was the leader of the UUUC and had the difficult task of holding together a wide range of unionist voices in parliament. The UUUC collapsed in 1977 when Molyneaux was critical of Paisley's involvement in an attempt to organise strike action in Northern Ireland. Molyneaux was now leader of the Ulster Unionist Party in Westminster and became the overall leader of the party in 1979 when West resigned this position.

In 1979 **Humphrey Atkins**, the secretary of state for Northern Ireland in **Margaret Thatcher's** new government, proposed round-table talks between the political parties in Northern Ireland. Molyneaux said the Ulster Unionist Party would not take part on the grounds that the proposals being put forward by Atkins for the governing of Northern Ireland would inevitably lead to a united Ireland.

Molyneaux was taken by surprise when Thatcher and Taoiseach **Garret FitzGerald** signed the **Anglo-Irish Agreement** in 1985. He had not anticipated that Thatcher would negotiate an agreement that would allow the Irish government to have a say in the affairs of Northern Ireland. Molyneaux united with Ian Paisley and the DUP to oppose the agreement, forming the **'Ulster says no'** campaign. A **day of action** was organised for 3 March 1986. The violence and intimidation that took place on that day was an embarrassment for Molyneaux and did little to stop the implementation of the agreement.

Gradually Molyneaux came to realise that the need for political negotiation was inevitable and that in order to avoid the Ulster Unionist Party from becoming absorbed into the DUP, more decisive action needed to be taken. In 1991 he allowed his party to take part in talks with the British government on the future of Northern Ireland and in 1992 he had a formal meeting in Dublin with Taoiseach **Albert Reynolds**.

Molyneaux contributed to the negotiations that led to the **Downing Street Declaration** in 1993. He supported the declaration but could not agree to the proposal that **Sinn Féin** be allowed to take part in peace talks. Molyneaux's leadership of the party came under pressure in 1995. Party members began to believe that Molyneaux was not taking sufficient advantage of the Conservative Party's reliance on Ulster Unionist Party support in parliament in his negotiations with the British government. He resigned as leader and was replaced by **David Trimble**.

Margaret Thatcher (1925–2013)

Margaret Thatcher was born in Grantham, Lincolnshire. In 1975 she became the first female leader of the **Conservative Party** and in 1979 she was elected the first female **prime minister of the United Kingdom**.

Before becoming prime minister, Thatcher had little involvement in political affairs relating to Northern Ireland. While leader of the opposition, she appointed her friend **Airey Neave** as **shadow spokesman on Northern Ireland**. Shortly before Thatcher took office as prime minister, Neave was killed when a bomb strapped underneath his car exploded outside the houses of parliament at Westminster. The paramilitary organisation, the **Irish National Liberation Army (INLA)**, claimed responsibility for the attack.

The first major crisis relating to Northern Ireland faced by Thatcher was the **hunger strikes** in 1981. **Provisional IRA** prisoners in the **H-blocks** of the **Maze Prison** refused food in protest at the removal of **special category status** from convicted prisoners. On 1 March 1981, Bobby Sands began the hunger strike and was soon joined by other prisoners. Sands died after sixty-six days without food and nine others also died of starvation. Thatcher was resolute in her determination not to give in to the demands of the hunger strikers, whom she viewed as criminals. The hunger strike was called off on 3 October 1981 and three days later the secretary of state for Northern Ireland, **James Prior**, announced that prisoners at the Maze could wear their own clothes.

One consequence of Thatcher's handling of the hunger strikes was that she became a target for the IRA. In October 1984, in an attempt to assassinate Thatcher, the IRA carried out a bombing of the Grand Hotel in **Brighton**, where the annual Conservative Party conference was taking place. Thatcher herself escaped injury but five others were killed, including a Conservative MP.

In the early 1980s there was continued frustration in the efforts to find a political solution to the crisis in Northern Ireland. An attempt by Thatcher's government to gradually devolve power to Northern Ireland was frustrated by opposition from the parties in Northern Ireland who were divided internally and against one another. The relationship between the Irish and British governments had been severely damaged by the hunger strikes and Taoiseach **Charles Haughey's** refusal to support Britain during the **Falklands War** in 1982. However, the increase in support for **Sinn Féin** in elections led to fears among the more moderate **SDLP** politicians and the British and Irish governments that a peaceful solution would become difficult to achieve.

Prompted by this development, in May 1983 the **New Ireland Forum** was established by the new Taoiseach, **Garret FitzGerald**. FitzGerald worked closely with the SDLP leader **John Hume** and other Irish political parties to come up with a number of proposals, which included: a **united Ireland**, with a single government for the island of Ireland; a **federal Ireland**, where Northern Ireland would have its own parliament within a united Ireland and a proposal for the **joint government** of Northern Ireland by London and Dublin. At a press conference with FitzGerald at an Anglo-Irish summit in November 1984, Thatcher rejected all of these proposals.

In spite of this setback, Thatcher was still motivated to continue negotiations with FitzGerald. The positions of the parties in Northern Ireland remained inflexible and it seemed that the only way to break the deadlock was to reach an agreement with the Irish government. Thatcher also believed that an agreement with Dublin would enable the British government to gain better control of the security situation in Northern Ireland.

At **Hillsborough Castle** on 15 November 1985, Thatcher and FitzGerald signed the **Anglo-Irish Agreement**. The agreement contained an acceptance of the principle that there would be no unity in Ireland without the consent of the majority in Northern Ireland and allowed for regular intergovernmental conferences between north and south.

The Anglo-Irish Agreement came as a surprise to all sections of unionist opinion, who had not anticipated that Thatcher would agree to the Irish government having a say in the affairs of Northern Ireland. Thatcher met with the Ulster Unionist Party leader **James Molyneaux** and the DUP leader **Ian Paisley**, who expressed unionist opposition to the agreement. Thatcher refused to make any concessions on changing its terms. A '**day of action**' was organised for 3 March 1986, but the widespread rioting that took place on that day had no impact in changing Thatcher's stance on the agreement.

Thatcher resigned as prime minister on 22 November 1990.

Seamus Heaney (1939–2013)

Seamus Heaney was born in Co. Derry and was brought up on the family farm of **Mossbawn** near Castledawson. He attended **St Columb's College** in Derry where **John Hume** was a fellow student. Heaney won a scholarship to **Queen's University Belfast** and graduated with an honours degree in English language and literature.

While studying and teaching in Belfast, Heaney became part of **the Belfast Group**, a writers' workshop that included other Northern Irish poets, including **Michael Longley** and later **Paul Muldoon**. In 1966, Heaney's first poetry collection, *Death of a Naturalist*, was published by Faber and Faber. The same year he was appointed English lecturer at Queen's.

Heaney supported the campaign of the civil rights movement in the late 1960s and knew many of those involved, including **Conn and Patricia McCluskey**. As a lecturer at Queen's, Heaney heard the speeches of the student activist **Bernadette Devlin**. He did not play an active role in the civil rights movement and as the situation in Northern Ireland became more violent, Heaney faced the challenge of whether or not to respond to the Troubles in his poetry.

In the late 1960s and early 1970s Heaney's reputation as a poet was established in Britain and America. In 1970, Heaney and his young family moved to California, where Heaney worked as a visiting lecturer at **Berkeley**.

In 1972 they returned to a worsening situation in Northern Ireland, when the **Bloody Sunday** shootings occurred in Derry in January and the **Bloody Friday** IRA bombings took place in Belfast in July. Heaney resigned his position as lecturer at Queen's and moved with his family to **Glanmore, Co. Wicklow**. Heaney strongly rejected criticism that he left Northern Ireland to escape the Troubles.

As a poet, Heaney dealt indirectly with the violent events that occurred in Northern Ireland in the 1970s and 1980s. In the sequence of 'bog poems' in the collection *North* (1975), for example, Heaney described the ritual killings of ancient people such as the **Tollund Man** in Denmark in a way that hinted at the violent deaths that occurred during the Troubles.

In 1984, Heaney was made a professor at **Harvard University** and in 1989 he was appointed professor of poetry at **Oxford University** for five years. As well as producing numerous collections of poetry, Heaney wrote works of literary criticism, edited anthologies of poetry and translated works into English from original languages, including ancient Greek, Irish and Old English.

Heaney was awarded the **Nobel Prize for Literature** in 1995.

Glossary

Useful Terms

Chapter 1

Dominion status According to the Anglo-Irish Treaty (1921), the newly created Irish Free State would be self-governing but would remain part of the British Commonwealth (empire).

Guerrilla warfare Fighting by a small independent group, often against regular soldiers.

Internment Imprisonment without trial.

Plenipotentiary A representative of a government given full power to act as they see fit on behalf of their government, often when in a foreign country.

Republic A state in which power is held by the people through their elected representatives, and which has an elected president rather than a monarch.

Chapter 2

Franchise The right to vote in an election.

Infrastructure Facilities such as roads, airports and energy supplies that help businesses and factories to function.

Loyalist A more extreme type of unionist. Loyalists strongly support the union between Great Britain and Northern Ireland and have a firm attachment to Protestant and British cultural heritage.

Republican A more extreme type of nationalist. Republicans believed that the situation in Northern Ireland could be resolved only by the end of partition and the creation of a thirty-two county Irish republic. Many republicans were willing to use violence in order to achieve this.

Chapter 3

Higher education Education that takes place after secondary school at a university or college.

Cabinet A group of senior government ministers and the prime minister who meet regularly to discuss government policy and make decisions.

Chapter 4

Cross-community In Northern Ireland this refers to when both the Catholic and Protestant communities are involved in a particular event, issue or project.

Whip This ensures that all members of a political party vote in line with party policy on important issues. A party official ('the whip') instructs members to vote in a particular way. Any party member who votes against the whip can be expelled from the party.

Chapter 5

Commemoration This is a way of remembering events from the past. Commemoration usually involves the participation of members of the public and can take different forms, for example a memorial plaque or monument, a formal ceremony, a parade, etc.

Depose To remove someone from office by force, such as overthrowing a king or queen.

Effigy A three-dimensional representation of a person. An effigy can sometimes take the form of a caricature of the person and is often burned.

Ritual In the case of the Apprentice Boys of Derry, a ritual is an action that took place at a specific time and place to commemorate the events of the siege of Derry.

Siege A military operation in which enemy forces surround a town, cutting off essential supplies.

Chapter 6
Royal Ulster Constabulary (RUC) This was the police force of Northern Ireland, formed in 1922. Membership of the police force was mostly Protestant.

Chapter 7
Internment Imprisonment without trial.

Marching season A period every year in Northern Ireland when members of organisations such as the Orange Order and the Apprentice Boys of Derry take part in parades across Northern Ireland.

Paramilitary organisation An organisation for which civilians organise themselves in the style of an army. Such organisations are often illegal and in Northern Ireland they included dissident groups such as the Provisional Irish Republican Army (IRA) and the Ulster Defence Association (UDA).

Chapter 8
Consensus Where different individuals or groups have opposing views but manage to reach an agreement that is acceptable to all parties.

Green paper A discussion paper published by a government. It usually contains an outline of a particular issue and puts forward for debate ideas on how to resolve this issue.

Power-sharing A system of government where political parties with opposing views agree to form a government together, known as an executive. This system allowed for the special circumstances of Northern Ireland. Power-sharing meant that unionist and nationalist representatives would govern Northern Ireland together. This allowed nationalists – traditionally a minority group in Northern Ireland – to have a strong voice in government.

Self-determination The right of a people to determine their own national identity.

White paper A policy document published by a government. It contains a formal statement of government policy on a particular issue.

Chapter 9
Partition The border dividing the 26 counties of the south of Ireland from the six counties of the north of Ireland, first introduced in 1921.

Reconciliation A healing of divisions between two sides.

Key Concepts

Bigotry: Showing intolerance towards a particular religion or the beliefs of a particular cultural group.

Civil rights: The right of citizens to be treated equally under the law, for example the right to vote or the right to equal access to government services. Civil rights emerged as a key issue in Northern Ireland in the 1960s, when practices that discriminated against Catholics were identified, including the use of gerrymandering, an unfair franchise system in local elections and an unfair system in the allocation of public housing.

Cultural identity: A sense a person has that they belong to a particular group. This is often to do with a person's nationality, ethnicity and religion. In Northern Ireland there is a strong connection between religion and national identity. Traditionally, people who belong to the Protestant religion identify as British and those who belong to the Catholic religion identify as Irish.

Cultural traditions: The rituals, practices and events associated with a particular group. Cultural traditions enable a group to create, express and reinforce a sense of cultural identity. For the Protestant community in Northern Ireland, examples of cultural traditions include the strict observation of the Sabbath (Sunday) and parades by loyal orders such as the Orange Order and Apprentice Boys of Derry. For the Catholic community in Northern Ireland, examples of cultural traditions include the use of the Irish language and the playing of Gaelic games.

Ecumenism: A movement to create better understanding between Christian churches. It seeks to focus on what Catholic, Protestant and Orthodox churches have in common rather than what separates them. It came to prominence after the Second Vatican Council in the 1960s, which called for unity among Christians. In Northern Ireland ecumenism was strongly opposed by Ian Paisley and his supporters.

Gerrymandering: The redrawing of borders of electoral areas to suit the interests of a particular group. It is used to enable a smaller political group to obtain a victory over a larger political group. In Northern Ireland, gerrymandering was used in areas where there was a majority nationalist population. Electoral borders were manipulated in such a way that unionist candidates could win control of local councils and be elected to the Northern Ireland parliament.

Power-sharing: A system of government where political parties with opposing views agree to form a government together, known as an executive. This system allowed for the special circumstances of Northern Ireland. Power-sharing meant that unionist and nationalist representatives would govern Northern Ireland together. This allowed nationalists – traditionally a minority group in Northern Ireland – to have a strong voice in government.

Propaganda: The spread of information to promote a particular political cause or point of view. The use of propaganda was widespread in Northern Ireland during the Troubles. It was used by political parties and paramilitary organisations on both sides of the nationalist and unionist divide.

Sectarianism: Division between religious groups. It can take the form of prejudice, discrimination or hatred towards a particular religion. In Northern Ireland, sectarian divisions have occurred between the Protestant and Catholic communities.

Terrorism: Acts of violence against civilians and security forces carried out in pursuit of political aims. During the Troubles in Northern Ireland, acts of terrorism were carried out by republican paramilitary organisations, such as the **Provisional IRA** and the **INLA** and by loyalist paramilitary organisations, such as the **UDA** and the **UVF**. Acts of terrorism took many forms, including detonating bombs and shooting incidents.

Tolerance and intolerance: Tolerance is when a person respects the beliefs and opinions of others, even if they do not hold these beliefs and opinions themselves. Intolerance is where a person does not respect the beliefs and opinions of others that differ from their own.

Useful Books and Websites

Useful Books and Articles

Bardon, Jonathan, *A History of Ulster*, Blackstaff Press, 1992.

Curran, Frank, *Derry: Countdown to Disaster*, Gill and Macmillan, 1986.

Currie, Austin, *All Hell will Break Loose*, O'Brien Press, 2004.

Devlin, Bernadette, *The Price of my Soul*, André Deutsch, 1969.

Dorr, Noel, *Sunningdale: the Search for Peace in Northern Ireland*, Royal Irish Academy, 2017.

Farrell, Michael, *Northern Ireland: the Orange State*, Pluto Press, 1990.

Farren, Seán (ed.), *John Hume: In His Own Words*, Four Courts Press, 2017.

Farren, Seán and Mulvihill, Robert, *Paths to a Settlement in Northern Ireland*, Colin Smythe, 2000.

Faulkner, Brian, *Memoirs of a Statesman*, George Weidenfeld and Nicolson, 1978.

Fisk, Robert, *The Point of No Return: the Strike which Broke the British in Ulster*, André Deutsch Limited, 1975.

FitzGerald, Garret, *All in a Life,* Gill and Macmillan, 1991.

Hennessey, Thomas, *Northern Ireland: the Origins of the Troubles*, Gill and Macmillan, 2005.

Hume, John, 'Transforming the Union: an evolving dynamic' in *Britain and Ireland: Lives Entwined* (vol. III), British Council Ireland, 2008.

Lacy, Brian, *Siege City: the Story of Derry and Londonderry*, Blackstaff Press, 1990.

Lee, J.J., *Ireland 1912–1985: Politics and Society*, Cambridge University Press, 1990.

McBride, Ian, *The Siege of Derry in Ulster Protestant Mythology*, Four Courts Press, 1997.

McCann, Eamonn, *War and an Irish Town*, Penguin, 1974.

McKittrick, David and McVea, David, *Making Sense of the Troubles*, Penguin, 2012.

O'Brien, Gerard, '"Our Magee Problem": Stormont and the Second University' in Gerard O'Brien (ed.), *Derry and Londonderry History and Society*, Geography Publications, 1999.

Ó Dochartaigh, Niall, *From Civil Rights to Armalites: Derry and the Birth of the Irish Troubles*, Cork University Press, 1997.

O'Doherty, Malachi, *Gerry Adams: an Unauthorised Life*, Faber and Faber, 2017.

O'Driscoll, Dennis, *Stepping Stones: Interviews with Seamus Heaney*, Faber and Faber, 2008.

O'Neill, Terence, *The Autobiography of Terence O'Neill*, Hart Davis, 1972.

Stanfiel, Heather, *The Walker Testimonial and Symbolic Conflict in Derry*, Four Courts Press, 2018.

Walker, Brian, 'Remembering the siege of Derry: the rise of a popular religious and political tradition, 1689–1989' in William Kelly (ed.), *The Sieges of Derry*, Four Courts Press, 2001.

Online Sources

The **RTÉ Archives website**, www.rte.ie/archives, contains a number of useful resources for studying this period. They include:

▸ An online exhibition, 'Civil Rights in Northern Ireland'. The exhibition includes audio and film clips relating to key events in the development of the civil rights movement such as the NICRA march in Derry on 5 October 1968 and the People's Democracy march in 1969

▸ Profiles of important individuals relating to this period, including William Craig, Austin Currie, Bernadette Devlin, Brian Faulkner, Seamus Heaney, John Hume, Eddie McAteer, Terence O'Neill and Ian Paisley

▸ Film clips relating to the **Apprentice Boys of Derry**, including the rioting in Derry in August 1969 and tension over Apprentice Boys parades in the 1980s

▸ Film clips relating to the **Sunningdale Agreement**, including reports on the negotiation and signing of the agreement in December 1973 and a report on the impact of the general strike in May 1974.

The **Scoilnet website**, www.scoilnet.ie, contains a number of resources for students studying this period. There are worksheets available based on the RTÉ archives online exhibition, 'Civil Rights in Northern Ireland'.

The **Conflict Archive on the Internet (CAIN) website**, www.cain.ulster.ac.uk contains a wealth of resources. They include:

▸ Articles and book extracts giving information on the background to the conflict in Northern Ireland

▸ Material relating to the **Sunningdale Agreement**, including a chronology of key events and links to extensive primary source material

▸ Primary source material relating to the **Coleraine University controversy** from the Public Record Office of Northern Ireland (PRONI), accessible through the CAIN website.

Newspaper articles are a useful source of information. Relevant newspaper archives include www.irishtimes.com/archive and www.irishnewsarchive.com. Both of these websites can be accessed free of charge through the Schools Broadband Network.

The Documents-Based Questions Examined

What is the documents-based question?

Section I on your Leaving Certificate history paper is the documents-based question. This question is compulsory and is worth 100 marks, i.e. 20 per cent of your overall mark.

For 2022 and 2023 the question will be based on one of the three case studies from *Later Modern Ireland: Topic 5 – Politics and Society in Northern Ireland, 1949–1993*. They are:

- The Sunningdale Agreement and the power-sharing executive, 1973–1974
- The Coleraine University controversy
- The Apprentice Boys of Derry.

In this section you will be given two sources drawn from **one** of the three case studies. They could be written sources such as a newspaper article, a political speech or an extract from a book, or visual sources such as a photograph or a political cartoon. Both sources will be about the same theme or event in the case study.

What types of question will be asked?

You will be asked to answer **four** types of question about these sources.

1   Comprehension

Usually there are three or four parts to this question at Higher Level and five at Ordinary Level. They are designed to test your understanding of the sources.

This is the most important question for Ordinary Level students, who can earn 40 out of 100 marks for it. For Higher Level students it is worth 20 marks.

> Some examples of the type of question:
>
> - In Document A, what is meant by . . . ?
> - What is the message of the cartoon (Document B)?
> - According to Document A, what role does . . . play in events?

2 Comparison

There are two parts to this question. They ask you to compare or note differences between the way the two sources deal with the event. You must refer to both sources in your answer or you will lose marks.

This question is worth 20 marks at both Higher and Ordinary Levels.

> Some examples of the type of question:
> ▸ How does the account of the event in Document A differ from the account in Document B?
> ▸ Which document is more effective in communicating its message?
> ▸ Comment on the portrayal of . . . in Documents A and B.
> ▸ Which document is more sympathetic to . . . ?

3 Criticism

There are two parts to this question. You may be asked to detect bias, propaganda, opinions or to make judgements about the reliability of the sources.

This question is worth 20 marks at both Higher and Ordinary Levels.

> Some examples of the type of question:
> ▸ Do you find bias in this document?
> ▸ How reliable is Document A?
> ▸ What are the strengths and weaknesses of Document B as a historical source?
> ▸ Is a political cartoon such as Document A a reliable source of historical evidence?
> ▸ Is Document B a primary or secondary source? Explain your choice.
> ▸ Do you agree that Document B is a good example of propaganda?
> ▸ Would you agree that Document B is an objective source?

It is really important that for the above three types of question you make use of evidence from the source(s) in your answer. Use words or phrases from the documents, name figures in cartoons or mention facts the sources refer to in your answer.

4 Contextualisation

This is the final question and it will ask about your background historical knowledge of the case study. Answering it will involve knowing about elements of the topic (*Politics and Society in Northern Ireland, 1949–1993*) that are relevant to the case study.

This is the most important question for Higher Level students as it is worth 40 marks out of 100. They should write a short essay of about one and a half pages. For Ordinary Level students it is worth 20 marks. One page will be enough at Ordinary Level.

It is probably best to do Section I first on your paper. But be very conscious of time. Remember, you have another three sections to deal with, so do not write too much for any of the four parts and do not spend more than 45 minutes on this section.

Questions to Ask When Examining a Source

SUMMARY: THE DOCUMENTS-BASED QUESTION

Type of question	Number of parts	Marks – Higher Level	Marks – Ordinary Level
1 Comprehension	3 or 4 short questions – Higher 5 questions – Ordinary	20	40
2 Comparison	2 short questions	20	20
3 Criticism	2 short questions	20	20
4 Contextualisation	1.5 pages – Higher 1 page – Ordinary	40	20

Does it contain opinions?

What event is the source about?

How well does it get its message across?

How is this source useful?

When and why was it made?

Who made the source?

Is it a primary or secondary source?

Was it made close to the event or many years later?

Is it an eye-witness account?

Are there any weaknesses such as bias?

Is the source reliable?

References

Chapter 1

1 Jonathan Bardon, *A History of Ulster* (Belfast: The Blackstaff Press, 1992), p. 539.

Chapter 2

1 Thomas Hennessey, *Northern Ireland: the Origins of the Troubles* (Dublin: Gill and Macmillan, 2005), p. 67.

Chapter 3

1 http://stormontpapers.ahds.ac.uk/pageview.html?volumeno=46&pageno=#bak-46-863
2 Frank Curran, *Derry: Countdown to Disaster* (Dublin: Gill and Macmillan, 1986), p. 27.
3 Gerard O'Brien, 'Our Magee Problem: Stormont and the second university', in Gerard O'Brien (ed.), *Derry and Londonderry: History and Society* (Dublin: Geography Publications, 1999), p. 679.

Chapter 4

1 *Derry Journal*, 9 February 1965.
2 *Derry Journal*, 19 February 1965.
3 O'Brien, 'Our Magee Problem', p. 685.
4 Frank Curran, *Derry: Countdown to Disaster*, p.42.

Chapter 5

1 Heather Stanfiel, *The Walker Testimonial and symbolic conflict in Derry* (Dublin: Four Courts Press, 2018), p. 26.

Chapter 6

1 Bardon, *A history of Ulster*, p. 653.
2 Frank Curran, *Derry: Countdown to Disaster*, p. 129.
3 Brian Walker, 'Remembering the siege of Derry: the rise of a popular religious and political tradition, 1689–1989', in William Kelly (ed.), *The Sieges of Derry* (Dublin: Four Courts Press, 2001).

Chapter 8

1 Noel Dorr, *The Search for Peace in Northern Ireland: Sunningdale* (Dublin: Royal Irish Academy, 2017), p. 58.

Index

Note: Pages numbers in **bold** indicate photograph captions.